GUIDING THE READING PROCESS

Techniques and strategies for successful instruction in K-8 classrooms

DAVID BOOTH

Stenhouse Publishers

YORK, MAINE

Pembroke Publishers Limited

MARKHAM, ONTARIO

I am indebted to Larry Swartz
for his support of this project and especially for his work on the bibliographies.

©1998   Pembroke Publishers
        538 Hood Road
        Markham, Ontario, Canada L3R 3K9
        www.pembrokepublishers.com

Canadian Cataloguing in Publication Data

Booth, David
    Guiding the reading process

Includes bibliographical references and index.
ISBN 1-55138-100-1

1. Reading (Elementary). I. Title.

LB1573.B675 1998   372.4   C98-931628-9

Distributed in the U.S. by Stenhouse Publishers
431 York Street,
York, Maine 03909
www.stenhouse.com
U.S. ISBN 1-57110-318-X

Library of Congress Cataloging-in-Publication Data
Booth, David.
    Guiding the reading process: techniques and strategies for
successful instruction in K-8 classrooms / David Booth.
        p.   cm.
    Originally published: Markham, Ont.: Pembroke Publishers c 1998.
    Includes index.
    ISBN 1-57110-318-X
    1. Reading (Elementary). I. Title.
LB1573.B674   1999   99-33650
372.41'2—dc21   CIP

Pembroke gratefully acknowledges the support of the Department of Canadian Heritage.

Editor: Joanne Close
Cover Design: John Zehethofer
Cover Photography: Ajay Photographics
Typesetting: Jay Tee Graphics Ltd.

Printed and bound in Canada
9 8 7 6 5 4 3

Contents

Introduction

In my teaching over the years, I have worked with children in classrooms and in demonstration settings, with student teachers, and with teachers taking graduate courses in language arts and literacy. Some teachers have been engaged in action research projects, exploring ways to support the development of young readers. I am always struggling to place theory inside practice, and this book allowed me to examine and assess the current theories of teaching reading, supported by classroom practice and teacher reflection. The teaching of reading is a significant part of our schooling, and to help us continue to change as teachers we now have access to journals, texts, research documents, and books written by educational authorities internationally.

Effective school change in the teaching of reading occurs from the inside out, with a staff who understands the foundations of the reading process, and who incorporates techniques and strategies that will enable each child to achieve reading success. By describing, examining, and reflecting on our beliefs about teaching reading, we begin to set in motion the process of change in our classrooms, as we design and rework carefully considered programs that assist every child in becoming an effective reader and writer.

In this book, you will find a variety of teaching strategies that will be useful in building an inclusive reading program, including:

- descriptions of strategies for helping young readers with different reading abilities,
- suggestions for mini-lessons in reading techniques, from phonics to literature discussions,
- literacy events that promote thoughtful, meaning-making strategies,
- ideas and suggestions for incorporating new strategies and techniques into classroom activities,
- outlines and checklists to help assess, monitor, and report on children's reading progress;
- book lists and computer programs to build classroom resources that promote reading success for each child.

This book is organized around strategies and techniques that accomplish two goals: 1) supporting young readers on the journey toward becoming independent readers; and 2) providing teachers with a variety of means for working with young readers in one-to-one conferences, in collaborative groups, and as a community of readers. The act of reading is a complex and integrative process, and a technique that works effectively with one child in a particular context may not be as useful with a group of struggling readers in another setting. It takes a teacher – or a team of teachers – to assist in the process that will help a child to become a reader who can read both creatively and critically. Such a program relies on more than a group of reading activities applied at random: it takes dedicated and committed teachers who will incorporate these strategies into their teaching/learning curricula, so that all children will continue to grow as readers.

My colleague and friend, storyteller Bob Barton, says "that we stand on the shoulders of those who have gone before in order to see further." In discussing reading theory and practice, so many teachers, writers, and researchers have lifted us up so that we can add to our knowledge base of how to best support young children in becoming independent readers, and how to assist teachers in designing literacy programs that achieve our goal of reading success for all.

I am fortunate to have met, either in person or through their writings, such fine educators whose ideas have permeated the teacher discussions, both inservice and preservice sessions, resulting in this book of reading techniques and strategies. The list of reference books indicates the valuable range of writings that we have incorporated into our teacher development curriculum. I want to acknowledge especially the following authors whose words continually illuminate our writing:

- Irene Fountas and Gay Su Pinnell, whose book, *Guided Reading*, is the best account of guided reading practice with young readers that we have;

- Regie Routman, whose book, *Invitations,* is a detailed and comprehensive account of teaching literacy in today's classrooms;
- Nancie Atwell, whose book, *In the Middle,* sets the standard for literacy teaching in the middle grades;
- Gordon Wells, whose writings have provided us with a clearer understanding of the theories of language and literacy;
- Dame Marie Clay, whose Reading Recovery® Institute has clarified the process of assisting young readers in difficulty, and of teaching young readers in classrooms;
- Jan Wells and Linda Hart-Hewins, whose books, *Read It in the Classroom!* and *Phonics Too!,* give us practical information for working with young readers in elementary education;
- Aidan Chambers, whose book, *Tell Me,* sets out a framework for literature and responsive classrooms;
- Harvey Daniels, whose book, *Literature Circles,* clearly outlines how to organize group discussions about books in the classroom;
- Susan Schwartz and Maxine Bone, whose book, *Retelling, Relating, Reflecting,* creates a framework for supporting and involving children's responses in the literacy program;
- Lucy Calkins, whose book, *Raising Lifelong Learners,* for teacher and parents, deepens our commitment to supporting literacy growth in all children.

We grow in our reading knowledge in so many ways. Last year, the teachers at Wilkinson Public School organized an in-service course around literacy, and in conducting those sessions, I found the format and the structure for this book. Their questions, suggestions and practices helped me to develop a framework within which I could discuss the huge array of strategies open to teachers of reading in elementary schools. In another locale, Silverthorn Public School, the teachers chose literacy as their professional focus for the year, and I was fortunate to be part of some of their discussions. As well, several described elements of their programs for me, and helped me to categorize the dozens of ideas in this book.

I work with teacher candidates who are on their way to becoming teachers, and their inquiries and fresh approaches constantly encourage and redirect my own thinking and practice. Many of their ideas are found throughout the pages of the book, and I am indebted to their integrity and commitment to young children.

Of course, the colleagues and friends who fill our lives strengthen everything we do. A few of those I can thank publicly are: Clare Kosnik, Linda Cameron, Paula Stanovich, Andy Biemiller, Meguido Zola, Chuck Lundy, Bob Barton, Judy Sarick, Irene Fountas, Wendy Geoghegan, Rikie Schieven, and of course Larry Swartz. This book is a collaborative venture. As well, my thanks to Ken Wood for his help and to Joanne Close, Deborah Sherman and Cathy Pouliot of JayTee Graphics for their efforts to make the material look like a book.

Part I: Becoming a Reader

1: A Set of Beliefs for Teaching Reading

1. As teachers, we need to establish a reading community with the whole class, where children participate in the ongoing literacy life of the classroom, where they come to value reading and begin to support one another in developing the attitudes and strategies required as lifelong readers, and where we as teachers model and demonstrate the kinds of reading activities in which we believe.

2. We must encourage independent reading with each child, supporting every occasion for making meaning with print, and offering useful strategies for enabling reading success for all children. We need to recognize a child's independence at each stage of growth in the journey toward becoming a reader.

3. We should group and regroup children for different reading events so that their needs and interests can be met in a variety of teaching/learning situations, enabling readers to move forward in their reading development as they gain confidence and competence, and encouraging them to share their reading experiences with one another.

4. Children need to be immersed in a world of words – listening, discussing, exploring, experimenting, reading, rereading, and writing. Our classrooms need to reflect a literacy environment and demonstrate to children the power and importance of reading and writing.

5. We need to post relevant materials for the children, including their written work, important event notices, newspaper articles on topics they are examining, quotes of the day, school and community newsletters, posters, and flyers. We can encourage children to create word mobiles, murals, collages, and banners. Literacy encompasses other forms of media, including television, radio, and the Internet. We can use children's knowledge and interest in these media forms to foster their development in reading and writing.

6. We can connect writing activities to the reading process so that literacy development is strengthened holistically, and children recognize the reciprocity of the processes of reading and writing.

7. We can focus on building word power for reading success, increasing each individual's bank of sight words, offering useful strategies for recognizing unfamiliar words, and sharing the delight of linguistic word play.

8. We can help children discover effective comprehension strategies for constructing significant meanings when interacting with different types of text, authors, and books.

9. We must deepen and extend the children's personal responses to texts, encouraging them to make life connections with what they read in order to build critical and appreciative understanding, as well as extend their knowledge of how different texts work.

10. We need to organize and manage a comprehensive reading classroom, including literacy events across the curriculum, with opportunities for reading development as individuals, as part of a small group, and as part of the community as a whole. Schools need teams of teachers to design and implement programs that support each child's development over the years. Teacher demonstrations and mini-lessons are necessary to help children move toward success in reading.

11. We can incorporate satisfying, supportive, and enriching materials in our classrooms, continually building print and computer resources that enable children to grow and stretch as young readers, helping them to recognize the personal power that literacy success can provide.

12. We need to monitor, track, assess, and reflect upon the children's reading progress in order to develop teaching and learning strategies that will help each child grow as a reader.

13. We need to assess and reassess our program of reading instruction by continuing to read, write, share, and research as professionals. We need to be aware of the experiences, ideas, and strategies of others, as well as conduct our own classroom inquiries, in order to modify, extend, and revise our methods of assisting young readers.

14. We need to communicate and co-operate with parents throughout the school year about their children's literacy development, accepting their concerns, sharing with them significant observations and data, and valuing their support at home and at school in building lifelong learners.

2: How Do We Learn to Read?

Some children seem to develop an understanding of reading and writing almost effortlessly. For others, the process is more challenging. Some children may recognize, for example, the sound of letters, but have trouble using other cues that will move them from analyzing individual words to implementing those cues in order to read fluently. Working together, we can help these children discover some of the "secrets" of reading.

Reading is a complex activity. How we approach and read a text depends on a number of factors, including the choice of text, reading ability, prior knowledge of the subject matter of the text, and the reasons for reading. Good readers bring a host of strategies to print and use them with discretion to make meaning. For example, a young reader may read ahead to confirm the meaning of a difficult word, reread, analyze the word, read words around it, and hypothesize and confirm predictions using all the cues available.

When working with children, we need to ensure that the text they are reading reflects their reading ability and experience, at the same time that it extends their learning by helping them to confirm existing knowledge, develop new strategies, increase their vocabulary, and expand their content background. Useful texts allow children to make predictions about what they will be reading and help them to focus on the ideas expressed by the author. Texts that are too challenging will force children to focus on individual words at the expense of the reading experience. Such a process does little to entice them to read, let alone permit them to find satisfaction in the experience.

Once children have selected an appropriate text to read, often with our assistance, we need to ensure that they have support before, during, and after their reading. Children need time to think about what they have read, to relate their reading to past knowledge, to formulate questions as they are reading, and to share their reading with others, first through discussions, then perhaps through art, or writing, or discussion. All of these activities extend children's learning and reinforce the notion that reading is an important source of information and satisfaction. A primary goal of our classrooms should be to establish a safe, supportive environment in which children can sample books, discover their reading tastes, extend their reading experiences, build their reading skills, and view themselves as members of a dynamic literary and literate community.

1. Children who are becoming readers need numerous opportunities to experience a variety of forms of literature – alphabet books, pattern books, non-fiction selections such as magazine and newspaper articles, poems, short stories, and novels.
2. Discussions and conferences – individual, small, or large-group – can help us lead children into exploring a text, and help develop their knowledge of how story works. Why do they think the author wrote this book? What does the cover tell us about the story? What do we know about the topic of the book? Have we read other books like this one? How do the books compare?
3. Reading vocabulary develops through a number of activities and opportunities, including:
   - participation in shared reading experiences – before children can match letters to corresponding spoken sounds they need to hear the words read aloud;
   - numerous occasions for reading a variety of texts that contain enough familiar words so the children are ensured of success, while at the same time the texts need to contain sufficient new words to challenge young readers and add to their reading development;
   - opportunities for discussing environmental print found in and out of the classroom – children learn common signs and symbols through repeated exposure;
   - participation in shared writing, where children can see the symbols that represent the sounds they hear written as they are spoken, and apply their learning in a supportive environment;
   - writing independently through the day, using words they have learned and consolidating their understanding of the sounds of language to corresponding letters written on a page.

For most people, reading is a vital part of life, both personally and in the work world. We need to establish environments and reading experiences in our classrooms that will help children develop competence as well as positive attitudes towards literacy. Young children, in particular, must have plenty of opportunities to read and meet with success early in their school years in order to appreciate the value of becoming independent readers.

The process of learning to read is similar to the process of learning to talk – both involve immersion in a language form. In the case of reading, children listen to stories read aloud, they read with family members and members of the class community, they read themselves, and they see others reading.

There are several crucial elements we can put in place to ensure a sound reading program: 1) an abundance of quality children's literature, fiction and non-fiction alike; 2) ample time for reading, writing, and discussion opportunities throughout the day; 3) guided reading experiences where print is examined and understood with care and precision; 4) varied reading sessions (independent, partner, small-group, whole-group, read-aloud); and 5) ongoing assessment to determine how we are facilitating the children's reading development.

Children need to experience effective models of writing to learn to read – from computer instructions to history books to adventure novels – to witness the numerous purposes of reading. Perhaps the strongest impetus of all in learning to read is the ability to pursue independently the work of a favorite author or a favorite genre. Supplying children with quality literature that reflects each child's reading interests and level of ability is one of the most important things we can provide. As well, experiencing a quantity of text materials reinforces the consistency of print conventions, sentence structure, and sound-letter patterns.

Reading and writing cross curriculum borders. We can seize teachable moments throughout the day as children take part in art activities, songs, or a social studies project. For young children, it is particularly important that they have plenty of chances for writing and relating their reading experiences to what they have written. All children need to talk about their experiences with a text. In this way, they come to see the value of their existing knowledge when reading related texts, and learn that they can apply their personal knowledge to predict and confirm meaning with any text they meet.

All reading programs require a range of reading configurations, from reading independently to sharing a book as a whole class. While most of us tend to read aloud to young children, we often assume that older children won't enjoy or benefit from the activity. Children, regardless of their age, grow from hearing literature read aloud. We have only to look at the proliferation of book tapes to appreciate the pleasure of listening to a story read aloud.

Finally, ongoing assessment and evaluation is a necessary component of a strong reading program. In order to design effective reading curricula, we need to know the progress of each child, his or her reading strengths and challenges, the strategies she or he uses, the child's use of the cueing systems, the types of books she or he wants and needs, and the child's attitudes towards reading.

We need to
- integrate reading and writing wherever and whenever possible,
- observe children's use of strategies and the nature of their interactions with the text,
- monitor the materials children read,
- assess and evaluate children's reading development on a regular basis,
- plan activities that reflect children's needs and foster their growth,
- help them to use their existing knowledge when reading a related text,
- create literature explorations that will whet their appetite for reading,
- help them to see themselves as valuable members of the literary community,
- increase each reader's sight vocabulary,
- teach the use of context cues to determine the meaning of new words, and phonetic information to determine their pronunciation,
- help them to make word analogies when they meet a word that is partly recognizable,
- have dictionaries and other support resources readily available,
- teach children to monitor and self-correct their reading whenever possible,

- encourage them to use words they have met in reading in their writing,
- create countless opportunities for reading and writing in a supportive environment.

The Cueing Systems

Reading is an interactive process in which the reader uses a variety of strategies for ensuring that comprehension occurs. In order to make meaning with print, all readers blend four cueing systems: pragmatic, semantic, syntactic, and phonographemic (phonics). Pragmatic and semantic cues help readers to anticipate the meaning of text; syntactic cues help readers to use syntax and language patterns to predict words and phrases; phonics cues help readers to test predictions for unrecognized or confusing words in order to construct or confirm meaning. It is important that we help young readers to become aware of how using the various cueing systems can help them find meaning in text and support their reading growth. Young children already have some of these strategies, and may use them to figure out individual words or phrases. The process is more complicated, however, when they must apply strategies to words embedded in a text, especially unfamiliar words within a text that is outside their frame of experience.

A reader uses the four systems simultaneously to varying degrees. Proficient readers use a minimum of cues, while less experienced readers or readers who are reading a text for a specific purpose may use more cues to help them determine meaning. In the former instance, readers rely mainly on prediction cues; in the latter instance, readers may use more visual cues, and may have to then reread the selection to confirm meaning and ensure comprehension.

Emergent readers may tend to use phonics cues as their primary strategy. When they are reading difficult texts, they, in essence, may be decoding the majority of words they meet. This limits the amount of comprehension that occurs as the result of the reading – the more a child must decode individual words in a text, the less meaning she or he may take away from the experience.

Semantic Cues (Knowing About the World)

The ability to decode words does not mean that one automatically understands the material decoded. A reader must be able to attach meaning to the words, to have some pre-existing knowledge of how this new textual information is integrated into their existing knowledge and experience base.

We can help children to develop their semantic cueing system by supplying them with print resources that tap into their worlds. As well, we can give children the opportunity to participate in discussions before and after reading, as they explore the topic, other works by the author and/or illustrator, other books in the series, the genre, and so on.

Children can make predictions about the book. As they read, they check their initial predictions and form new questions based on what they have read. In this way, children can see the role their existing knowledge plays in interpreting new ideas and words in print. For young children, this can be a powerful boost to their reading confidence – while they may not be fluent readers, they have knowledge that can help them to read the text.

Many of the activities we do with children in novel study, for example, explore the semantic cueing system: making a story map, creating a character sketch, defining the writer's style, identifying the mood. In addition, field trips, films, and newspapers, can be used to supplement the children's knowledge, thereby increasing their ability to call on semantic cues as a reader.

Syntactic Cues (Knowing About Language)

Syntactic cues are those that involve identifying the function – noun, verb, adjective, adverb, and so on – and the basic language patterns used in English. English is not a chaotic language; it is governed by structures regarding word use and how these words are used in sentences. Children who are able to use syntactic cues are those who, when they come upon an unknown word, read the sentence in order to know the type of word needed, and can approximate a guess based on this information. As their ability to discern visual and oral communication strengthens, they can use the more formal written constructions as their guide to determining what is needed in a sentence.

Phonographemic Cues (Knowing About Print)

Phonographemic (phonics) cues are those relating to the sounds we hear (individual letters, combinations of letters), the letters of the alphabet, and conventions of print. Although English comprises only 26 letters, there are more than 40 sounds. Since there are more sounds than letters in the alphabet, it can be said that English lacks a complete one-to-one correspondence between letters and sounds. Readers then, particularly proficient readers, tend to rely on semantic and syntactic cues.

Phonographemic cues, or phonics cues, are used extensively by early readers and readers who want to analyze an unknown word, or to confirm a guess or prediction. If a reader is fairly certain of what a word is, based on information gleaned from other cues such as reading words around the word, she or he can use phonics to analyze the letters and confirm the knowledge. For children who are unable to read the word, we can give them an additional cue by saying the sound of the first letter. Other children who are having difficulty mastering reading may benefit from focusing on aspects of sound-letter relationships such as consonants, consonant blends and digraphs, and long and short vowel sounds, and then applying this knowledge with actual text. We can help young readers to use phonics cues when necessary at the same time as we encourage their use of other cueing systems with authentic text.

Children appear to recognize letters in the following order: beginning consonants, final consonants, consonant digraphs, medial consonants, consonant blends, long vowels, and short vowels. They begin to see what a word looks like in print and the relationship between the sounds they hear and the symbols on the page. Many children come to school knowing the letters in their names – this can serve as the starting point for teaching. Children become aware of sound-letter correspondence through reading, particularly reading print that they hear and see in shared big books. We can help children to focus on familiar letters and letter patterns, and increase their knowledge of the sounds those clusters of letters make, through a variety of activities, such as reading songs, rhymes, and stories that focus on particular words. Together, we can explore words in a number of ways, including talking about particular aspects of a word, and noting other words that sound the same.

We can help children move forward by having them focus on the sounds of parts of words, as well as on individual letters. In this way, they can match their word with other words that share this pattern. With plenty of opportunities gained through reading and writing, children can apply their phonics knowledge to longer words. Fluent readers know how to break unfamiliar words into chunks, to look for compound words, prefixes and suffixes, and familiar letter clusters, then to use context to confirm their word analysis strategies. Young readers need demonstrations and conferences where these strategies are modelled so that they will become readers who incorporate all of the cueing systems in order to read fluently.

As children begin to understand the relationship between sounds and letters, they can demonstrate their understanding in their writing. Even invented spellings can help you to identify a child's level of development and help you to tailor your teaching to foster his or her growth with specific word patterns.

Pragmatic Cues (Knowing About Books)

Pragmatic cues refer to the appearance of a text, including how it looks on a page (e.g., a list versus a page from a novel), how it is organized (e.g., point form, headings), and how it functions. Young children learn that books are read from front to back and that text is read from left to right. While this information may seem very basic, it is instrumental in the reading process. We can discuss with the children the processes we use when reading a list or a poem: what is different when we read the two pieces? Identifying the genre of a text through its print characteristics may help children to determine how they will read the material and sets the stage for reading. For example, there are five small but interrelated stories in the book, such as in *Frog and Toad* books by Arnold Lobel. Are the stories connected? Do they interrelate? Do the characters change?

Creating a Strong Literary Program

With these elements in place, we can expect that all children should be reading independently at level by the end of the primary grades. If we develop strong literacy programs at the primary levels, we will dramatically reduce the number of reading problems experienced by today's adolescents and young adults. To do this, we need to focus on core elements of a program, including:

- alphabet knowledge,
- knowledge of sound-letter correspondences,
- automatic sight words,
- reading for meaning,
- numerous opportunities for reading many types of books,
- increased teaching time and extra resources devoted to at-risk readers,
- a secure environment that encourages children to grow as readers and writers.

3: Supporting Critical and Creative Comprehension

When we read, are we always able to make sense of what we are seeing in print? Do we connect to what the author is saying and do we think about what she or he is saying? Are the author's words or ideas too far removed from our own? The question remains for us as teachers: how can we assist children in making sense of what they read, so that their personal understanding and satisfaction will grow and deepen from the experience? This is what we mean by teaching comprehension.

Reading comprehension or textual understanding occurs when we are able to interpret written symbols in order to make meaning. A reader internalizes the accrued meanings and relates that to previous knowledge, experience, and texts read before. Comprehension is a cognitive, emotional process, and thus it is difficult to assess. Yet its presence or absence can be determined to some extent when we watch and listen to children reading a text; when we ask them to describe what they have read; when we discuss books that they are reading; and when we share their responses to what they have read.

These informal ways to assess children's comprehension can be combined with more formal assessments to provide us with a picture of the children's level of comprehension with a particular text. We can then assist children with strategies that enhance comprehension to help them make meaning before they read, as they read, and after they read. This section will help to connect comprehension to the widest frame of meaning making that we can create for the child.

4: The Importance of Response to Text

Response activities allow children to develop insights into other worlds – to notice and accumulate new words and language patterns, to learn to discuss an idea from a text with confidence, to analyze and form generalizations from texts, to apply new learning to their lives, and to become members of a literacy community. A good story provides a powerful context for looking at how words work. Limited readers, in particular, need to see the richness of literature response, and to recognize that a story is only a beginning point for expanding ideas and increasing language strengths. What children do after reading should relate to what they have read, from a simple retelling through writing in their dialogue journals.

Responding to What We Read

If we were able to observe the thought processes of fluent readers, we would notice that they think about a book before they open its cover, they draw on their knowledge base to identify the type of text and the strategies they will need to read it. As they begin to read, they watch for visual cues (e.g., pictures, subheadings, etc.), look for main ideas, confirm initial predictions, relate text to what they know, look for details that link to existing knowledge, anticipate what will come next, monitor for comprehension, use information from all cueing systems judiciously, and use contextual cues and occasionally word analysis to understand new words and concepts. After reading they need time to reflect on the text, to relate ideas to their lives, and to consider the implications of the author.

We want to support these behaviors in young readers, for these strategies ensure that they finish reading a text richer for the experience and with an expanded knowledge base on which they can draw. How we promote these behaviors in emerging readers is a more difficult concept.

We can begin by guiding children through a text, helping them to discover its secrets and its wonders, its similarities to other books they have read in terms of content, patterns, or structure, its connections to their personal world and to the world at large. Nothing that we do, see, read, learn, or experience is in isolation – we need to help children appreciate that books, too, connect to aspects of our personal lives, our body of knowledge, and the world around us. In this way, children will come to see themselves as readers and thinkers who move beyond decoding words on a page towards understanding what they have read, and the text's relationship to the world they are constructing.

It is crucial that we know children's interests and strengths, as well as their methods for making meaning: what they will read, the approach they take to the task of reading, the strategies they employ to help them read, how they receive our attempts at helping, and the degree to which they relate new information to old. In this way, we can extend their learning by helping them to develop more efficient strategies that will enable them to negotiate meaning making in a more efficient, deeper manner.

We want to help children develop into independent, purposeful readers who will think carefully about what they have read. Often, readers in trouble make little sense of what they have been decoding, or they choose to ignore meaning making completely, and give up in frustration as they fail at word calling. All children need effective comprehension strategies as they grow into independent readers and writers. We need to promote thoughtful interaction with what is being read so that readers will be able to select relevant, significant information from the text, make sense of it, and integrate that with what they already know into a personal construct of knowledge.

Meaning and Experience

Everyone's experience differs. We need to keep this reality in mind as we work with groups of children so that we don't present only one interpretation of a story. Instead, we must share our expertise in such ways that support the children but encourage their learning. In order for readers to understand a book, they must relate it to other books read and to life experiences, and combine the knowledge gained from this book to their knowledge base. The strength of these connections relates directly to the children's level of comprehension. If the children can't connect the reading to personal aspects of the lives, their level of comprehension will suffer just as it will if they can't connect the text to others they have read.

Recognizing and Seeking Patterns

A fluent reader's recognition of words is so immediate and vast that they rarely notice their use of context cues. Their rate of recognition is directly tied to the amount of reading they do – the more a reader reads, the greater the automatic sight vocabulary. A parallel situation exists for those who read a variety of types of text: as they increase their exposure to text types, their recognition of patterns and structures specific to a genre of text increases. That knowledge of patterns is reinforced when writing and reading are combined – children then have the opportunity to put into practice their awareness of how print works. However, fluent readers may sometimes miss interesting turns of phrases or special nuances because they are processing text at a speed that does not allow for subtleties. Revisiting or working with the text may increase both comprehension and the metacognitive awareness of experience of the text.

Setting the Stage

1. Establish a core set of resources for the classroom, including sets of books to be shared (e.g., novels, anthologies, collections), a selection of books for independent reading (e.g., novels, biographies), curriculum resources (e.g., texts, kits, media, computer programs).

Why Children Need to Respond

1. Children need the opportunity to explore all aspects of a text.
2. When children share responses, they further their knowledge and help to build a community of learners.
3. Response activities can help children to overcome areas of text they found challenging.
4. Response activities reinforce the goal of reading, which is to make meaning.
5. Response activities can be done on an individual basis, with a partner, or as part of a small group. All children can work in an environment that suits their particular needs.
6. Response activities can take the form of writing, drawing, painting, acting, sculpting, and performing. Children can choose a mode of response that reflects the text they have read.
7. Response activities help children to link their reading to other aspects of their life and learning.
8. Response activities provide children with the time they need and the opportunity to review what they have gained from reading a text.
9. Children can come to better appreciate what they have read – a text's language, its character sketches, the twists and turns of its plot.
10. Children can become more aware of universal truths that exist in literature, and in life.

2. To begin, we may use prepared resources (e.g., guides, manuals, activity booklets) that accompany books, anthologies, or readers. These offer starting points for literature exploration, and allow us to observe and work with each child as we personalize the activities.

3. We can begin by creating folders of follow-up activities for each selection (e.g., question guides, author information booklets, documents). Generic response activities can promote interpretation and word play.

4. We need to provide experiences that help children to access relevant knowledge before reading a text, to think about experiences they have had, or to organize their thoughts and opinions about what they are going to read.

5. We want to encourage children to engage in "grand conversations," to think and feel and respond to the issues, the characters, the events, and the language of the selection. The focus is on topics of interest to the participants, and everyone's opinions are significant when supported by the text. We can encourage children to share their thoughts and experiences with their classmates, extending the meaning making for everyone.

6. We need to integrate the language processes by ensuring that response activities provide opportunities for further reading, writing, speaking, and listening. Children need to use language to articulate their ideas and to interact with the thoughts and feelings of others.

7. At-risk readers require group members who will listen to one another, help activate background knowledge and build upon it, each learning from the other as they share and contribute ideas. By using a variety of grouping patterns, we can offer each child flexible settings for growth, ensuring that the purpose will determine the groupings. Heterogeneous groups, whole-class, and sometimes ability groups, offer children opportunities to develop particular skills and to engage in discussion and in activities with a variety of children who offer different strengths. For example, ESL children need to read, write, and talk in meaningful ways about texts in co-operative and collaborative settings that encourage interaction. They require a modelling of language by the participants engaged in using English for authentic purposes.

8. Literature can instill a love of reading, but not when it is accompanied by fragmented activities. Instead, activities need to be integrated, significant, and thoughtful in order to encourage children to consider and reflect upon what they have read long after the book has been closed.

9. The development of independent readers is best accomplished through the purposeful structuring of literacy experiences. We need to read to children several times during the day, to sometimes reread the same texts, and to provide time for the children to read. It is important for children to develop familiarity with a variety of texts, to reread passages and texts for the sake of developing fluency, and to read selected parts in order to develop varied reading responses to the text. Books may be selected that share a common element: author, structure, theme, time, different versions

of the same book with different setting, or contrasting views. Such structuring enables the developing independent reader to build a wider perspective and gain an increased awareness of the reading resources.

10. There are many ways in which children can describe and express their thoughts and opinions about a book they have read. In choosing words to describe a particular story or passage, the child's ability to think critically and make judgments is challenged and expanded. As the child is directed to important words within a text, focus on meaning is stimulated. For example, the construction of a word collage as a response encourages the child to make multifaceted connections to the material.

11. The development of writing skills in conjunction with reading response also assists the child to focus on literacy values and skills. Encouraging the child's response, however, remains a priority. The child's individuality of expression and interpretation is supplemented by the guidance, the encouragement, and the knowledge of the enabling adult.

12. Responses to literature may be personal within a group context. Sharing informal story "gossip" broadens the opportunity for children to express their opinions and perceptions about what they have read. The opportunity for discussion can be formal as well as informal, and we may facilitate the opportunity for different kinds of discussion by directing attention to specific aspects of the literature. What is of interest to each child, however, is a prime factor in extending the child's interest in literature through his or her responses to the form and content.

Teaching Tips
1. Provide a variety of response modes from which children can select.
2. Model and demonstrate examples of various response strategies.
3. Share, display, and discuss reading responses with the class.
4. Display examples of effective responses from previous classes.
5. Organize a class chart or schedule of reading activities each week
6. Design activities surrounding a specific author or illustrator.

---

7. Make a reading folder for each child. Children can record books read, and the type of response activity.
8. Establish reading contracts and schedules for conferences and group activities.
9. Encourage and negotiate with children to undertake a variety of response activities.

5: The Teacher's Role in Reading Acquisition

To maximize the children's time engaged in responding to text, we need to make them aware of the various ways they can react, the materials they can use to form their responses, and the variety of ways of sharing responses.

Before we do this, however, we need to help the children prepare for the reading by providing a context for it. We need to ensure the children are introduced to the text and know the strategies they need to read it. We need to allow sufficient time for children to explore the text, to read it, to think about its plot, characters, and setting, and to consider how they would like to share their reading concerns with others.

Children need to know that they will have time to reflect on their reading, and to decide on the most effective mode of creating their responses. We can help them to move from their independent reading to group sharing by discussing their choices and how they might shape their materials. On occasion, some children will tend to work using the same response mode. In these instances, we need to encourage children to experiment with other modes of response.

Part of the effectiveness of the responses rests on the atmosphere in the classroom. Children need to know that they can safely share their opinions, their perceptions, and ways in which they changed as a result of the reading with peers who will respect and consider what each member has to say. We need to monitor the class environment and show, through our attention to each child, the value we place on their learning.

6: The Stages of Reading

Children will want to become readers by having others read to them, by watching others read, by reading as part of a group, by reading independently, and by having someone listen to them as they read aloud. Most children follow what can be considered a continuum of reading acquisition; however, they do not always master skills in order. That is, they may have difficulty with one strategy, yet will have gained another typically evidenced by a more fluent reader. Competencies vary according to the text read and the situation in which the child finds himself or herself reading.

When we assess a child's reading ability, we need to consider where the majority of the behaviors fall on a particular place in the continuum. We need to watch that the child makes gains that will move him or her into the next stage of reading, but this cannot be done by comparing one child to another. Children progress at their own rate and in their own style. In the past, readers who progressed at a slower rate were often labelled (e.g., learning disabled, dyslexic, attention deficit disorder). If we identify the process that needs to be developed, however, then we have a much clearer picture of the problem and what the child needs to do to build strength as a reader.

Since reading is an individual process, one of the best indicators we can use to assess a child's growth is his or her development through the year. In order to do this, we need to establish a baseline of skills and knowledge. As we assess the child through the year, we return to the baseline to see where the child has made gains.

For children at each stage of reading, we need to:
- base our teaching on a sound theory of how children learn, in particular, how they learn to read,
- select texts that children can read successfully on their own and that will make them want to read other texts,
- assist children in using visual information, sound-letter correspondence, analogies, words within words, and so on,
- ensure that children read to make meaning and that they find significance in what they read,
- provide opportunities for children to read increasingly difficult texts,
- model the use of strategies for growing as a reader, and model the use of self-assessment strategies to monitor this growth,
- help children to connect the processes of reading and writing through co-operative writing activities and through the creation of significant written responses to what they have read.

The Early Reader

The early reader, who is sometimes referred to as the prereader, enters kindergarten with some of the skills and concepts she or he needs to become a young reader. These children enjoy reading, since most of their experiences with texts have involved being read to by family members or caregivers. Books, then, represent pleasure and entertainment for them. They like to read with someone, and they know that they will be entertained, informed, or amused by books – many children will have favorite stories they like to hear again and again. These readers have a sense of story and enter into it readily.

The children will often pick up a book and approximate reading, holding it the right way, stopping the reading while they turn the page, and finishing the story exactly on the last page. Such imitation is not without value. Children learn that texts give readers cues to reading, that print on a page matches certain words, that pictures support the story, that books are read from front to back, that text flows from left to right, that reading is an authentic activity. When children "read" books in this way, they are preparing themselves to become readers.

Children know that print carries meaning, and they are aware of sources of print around them – in books, on street signs, on products, on labels, on signs. While they recognize many of these words in context, they may not carry over this knowledge when they see the words in isolation. These readers may not know how sounds are represented by letters. Phonemic awareness – how sounds combine to make words, and phonics – how words are written on a page – will develop during this period.

Phonics instruction, if it is to be effective, should occur through real reading activities, such as using rhymes, songs, patterns and word games.

These activities focus children's attention on sounds and the corresponding letter or letters that represent them. It is only when children have a knowledge of sound-letter correspondence that they can begin to read and write independently and transfer knowledge from one situation to another. The use of phonics instruction drills, while useful in determining a child's awareness of some aspects of phonics, may not help him or her develop the knowledge a reader needs when those words or sentences are used in real texts.

Characteristics of the Early Reader

- knows that books represent pleasure and that they are entertaining,
- has favorite stories that can be read repeatedly and still capture the child's attention,
- participates in reading familiar books,
- chooses to read alone or with friends,
- mimics how a parent or teacher reads the book – holds it correctly, turns pages, knows beginning and end of text,
- tries to match spoken words to written words in familiar pattern books,
- expects that pictures will support the text,
- uses pictures to predict meaning,
- possesses sight vocabulary, including common words on packaging, the names of restaurant chains, words on street signs, product names,
- recognizes some sight words in context,
- recognizes own name and letters in his or her name,
- cannot decode unfamiliar words,
- knows that writing represents meaning,
- when writing, imitates shapes of letters by using straight and rounded lines,
- has yet to develop much phonemic awareness,
- is curious about environmental print,
- sees himself or herself as a reader.

The Emergent Reader

An emergent reader, like the early reader, enjoys listening to stories and has favorite books that she or he seemingly never tires of. Children at this stage know that books can provide them with entertainment and information and they see themselves as capable of reading them. These youngsters have refined their knowledge of how books work, and realize that the purpose of print can be to record or share meaning, and that it is

---

Characteristics of the Emergent Reader

- shows interest in literature read aloud,
- voluntarily selects and shares books,
- enjoys texts with vivid illustrations,
- connects visual images to text,
- initiates independent reading of favorite books,
- chooses books of appropriate difficulty,
- is beginning to recognize different authors' styles,
- still needs some support with unfamiliar texts,
- relates sequences of events from personal stories or stories she or he has heard,
- relates print to personal experience,
- echoes recognized passages,
- retells past experiences,
- reads back short experience stories dictated to a teacher,
- appreciates personal talk written down and read by others,
- makes meaningful predictions using semantic and syntax clues,
- likes to verbalize stories when watching video,
- demonstrates confidence when silently reading along to audiotapes,
- likes to listen to familiar favorite stories, rhymes, jingles, and songs,
- uses literature as a framework for dramatic play, exploring rhythmical language patterns, painting, sculpting, movement, and music,
- understands print directionality,
- identifies and names most letters,
- recognizes some common words as well as some environmental print (about 20 words) out of context,
- follows a line of print in an enlarged text,
- realizes that print has common or fixed meaning,
- understands function and power of print,
- attempts to write using consonant sounds, familiar patterns, and images,
- experiments with forms,
- role-plays reading using oral language, writing, painting, symbols, sounds, movement,
- uses initial letters, along with meaning and other cues, to figure out words and correct errors,
- is beginning to understand what reading can do for him or her,
- represents many words with invented spelling.

---

fixed. They are beginning to rely on semantic and syntactic cueing systems to predict events, and can retell sequences of events. These children are interested in developing their print abilities. They like to have their stories transcribed, which they can read back to the teacher or parent.

To help them develop knowledge of how writing reflects spoken words, we need to create environments where children are surrounded by print. We need to show examples of how print is used and give them plenty of opportunities to read books successfully, particularly pattern books and books with detailed illustrations. Shared reading, of course, brings these books alive and directs children to focus on functions of print. Finally, publishing the children's own stories gives them real reasons to write and reinforces the purpose of writing – to record and to share.

The Developing Reader

This reader can read some texts independently and successfully. Children at this stage of reading often enjoy books by a favorite author, including books in a series, and it is during this period that children come to recognize characteristics of various genres. With this knowledge and their experience in reading, they begin to develop a personal literary taste.

Their knowledge of sound-letter correspondence is growing, and they can recognize and write letter groups such as blends and digraphs. Their knowledge of sight words is also growing, and they can read these words in both familiar and unfamiliar contexts.

As they read, developing readers use all four cueing systems to help them make meaning. They are able to self-monitor their reading, identifying and correcting miscues, and can substitute words that make sense when they are unsure of a text. At this level, children are reading silently. Some children may still fingerpoint or say the words softly to themselves. As their reading ability develops, they will discontinue these practices.

The Fluent Reader

The fluent reader has arrived at a point where she or he has built up an extensive sight vocabulary and thus is free from the time-consuming word analysis that may have occurred at previous stages. Fluent readers can read a range of texts for a variety of purposes, read silently, link new information with existing knowledge, and adjust

Characteristics of the Developing Reader

- is developing a strong sense of story,
- enjoys independent reading, particularly with familiar texts,
- discusses readings in small groups,
- values the connection of reading and writing,
- uses context cues to predict and make meaning,
- reads chapter books and simple novels,
- uses many reading strategies appropriately,
- retells plot events in sequence,
- describes characters,
- reads fluently some texts aloud,
- recognizes characteristics of various genres of texts,
- increases knowledge of literary elements and genres,
- reads silently for periods of time,
- reads and finishes a variety of materials with guidance,
- periodically self-corrects,
- makes substitutions when text doesn't make sense,
- pays close attention to print for decoding purposes,
- recognizes phonic generalizations – digraphs, blends, rhyming words,
- has a growing sight vocabulary,
- reads and understands most new words,
- uses, with guidance, reference materials to locate information.

their style of reading to reflect the type of book being read.

This is a critical stage in reading. Some children may begin to lose their enthusiasm for reading because books may appear too challenging, or they no longer find themselves as captivated by story. In these cases, we must choose books that children enjoy and that they can read successfully, all the while avoiding habits and classroom routines that may give reading activities the appearance of a chore (e.g., routine comprehension questions). Children need to confirm reading as an act that entertains them, that brings them satisfaction, that adds to their knowledge, and that is undertaken for genuine reasons.

Just as they are becoming independent in their reading, so, too, are they becoming independent in their writing. These children are learning to write in a variety of forms for a variety of audiences and purposes. In addition, they are improving the quality of their written work through editing and proofreading, and are mastering the conventions of the language.

Our role is to help children develop those strategies that will increase their reading and writing fluency. We can do this in part by observing genres that appear challenging to children and by modelling demonstrations of behavior we consider useful (e.g., proofreading written material), by conferring with children on an as-needed basis, and by acting as a resource to help them rediscover the joys of reading.

Characteristics of the Fluent Reader

- selects and reads independently a range of texts (e.g., historical, humor, information, sports),
- takes time to read, and enjoys the experience,
- reads with the expectation of gaining new knowledge, which can be applied to future reading,
- reads critically,
- requests books by a favorite author,
- predicts events of a text based on prior knowledge and context,
- reads to make meaning and not just to identify all words,
- cites part of a text to support an opinion or assessment,
- shares opinion of fiction texts, their plot, characters, setting, use of literary devices, and so on,
- shares opinion of non-fiction texts, their quality of material, breadth of topic coverage, and so on,
- discusses the main ideas of the story with others who have read the book,
- discusses and evaluates the author's choices and point of view,
- identifies and discusses the purposes of a variety of genres,
- views the theme of a book in the context of personal and cultural beliefs,
- identifies and discusses current events and relates them to his or her own experience,
- shares confidently responses to a book,
- understands the language structures of the text,
- uses text components (e.g., table of contents, index) to facilitate reading,
- uses a variety of reading strategies,
- skims and scans where applicable,
- summarizes information succinctly,
- follows written instructions,
- self-monitors and corrects reading.

The Independent Reader

The independent reader reads texts independently and silently. The style of reading reflects the material being read, and the readers monitor their reading for understanding.

These children can read a range of books, as well as novels that reflect other cultures, other times, and other ways of looking at the world. They are capable of interpreting complex plots and characterization and need to be challenged to move ahead on their own, using fiction, non-fiction materials, and computers.

Characteristics of the Independent Reader

- reads independently complex material,
- begins to interpret more deeply materials read,
- reads silently with ease,
- chooses books according to needs, abilities, interests,
- prepares for reading by drawing on prior knowledge and by analyzing the text to be read,
- reads and thinks critically – questions author's use of vocabulary, devices, etc.
- predicts accurately unfamiliar words,
- confirms predictions, makes educated guesses,
- creates mental images to visualize descriptions,
- makes meaning through syntactic patterns, idioms, imagery, multiple word meanings,
- absorbs diversity of meanings through discussion and analysis,
- paraphrases, predicts, anticipates, and reads ahead for additional content,
- rereads for clarification purposes or to relate new knowledge to existing knowledge,
- enjoys responding to reading – talking, writing, illustrating, role-playing,
- has a well-developed sense of narrative and its diverse forms,
- recognizes a variety of writing styles,
- enjoys writing "in the style of,"
- builds a coherent, personal interpretation of the book,
- connects the book to the real world,
- reads prepared texts aloud,
- self-monitors for understanding,
- self-corrects when necessary,
- tests hypotheses,
- analyzes unfamiliar words for roots, prefixes, and suffixes.

To further their development, we can encourage them to read a range of texts in a variety of ways, including independent reading, shared reading, and in literature circles. Their writing often reflects their reading knowledge, and they can be encouraged to respond to texts read in innovative ways.

The "English as a Second Language" Reader

These readers face a special challenge. Although they share their peers' reading tastes, their level of English precludes them from reading many age-appropriate texts. High-interest, low-vocabulary novels were developed to fill this gap, but did not prove to be a great success, with a general lack of plot and character sophistication. As well, few children want to read a book that is read by younger children. What do we give these children that will appeal to their humor, their sense of adventure, and their thirst for story? How do we teach them to read?

First, we need to realize that it is important to honor their culture. We can provide an atmosphere where they see their past experiences as valuable to their learning of English: these children have in place a set of skills and a knowledge bank on which they can draw as they learn English. They may benefit from being able to speak and write in their home language as they become accustomed to their new surroundings.

Secondly, we need to welcome these children into the school and make them feel a part of the school culture. If a child has no English language, we can pair him or her, if possible, with a child who shares the same home language. This buddy can introduce the new child to the physical layout of the school, its schedule, its resources, and its extracurricular activities.

Thirdly, we cannot offer ESL readers lower-level texts. Instead, we can give these children the same books as others are reading, then structure the learning so that they can have assistance and support as they read. This can be done by including the following components in the reading program:

- pair the ESL reader with another child in the class,
- pair the child with a buddy reader, preferably another ESL reader, who has developed reading ability in English and can foster the reading skills of a younger ESL reader,
- include plenty of demonstrations for the entire group so that the ESL reader does not feel that she or he has been singled out,
- include a range of reading materials that reflect and honor other cultures,
- provide a range of reading experiences, including shared reading, guided reading, and group read alouds where the child can experiment without a fear of failure,
- tape stories and novels children are reading and make these tapes available to all children so they can use them as needed,
- encourage the ESL reader to complete written responses with a partner or as a member of a small group,
- incorporate writing as a basis for their literacy learning,
- make the child aware of response forms that do not rely only on writing, such as drama and visual arts,
- make parents a part of the child's reading program by discussing strategies and goals of the program, and what they can do to help their child read at home.

7: A Framework for Reading Instruction

1. Reading Aloud
The teacher reads aloud to the children – in large groups, in small groups, to individuals, to explore stories, patterns, and words that are challenging, that connect to other books, that demonstrate the satisfaction found in reading.

2. Shared Reading
Children read together (often using a big book), rereading, retelling, innovating on the patterns, and attending to interesting or unfamiliar words.

3. Shared Writing

The teacher writes with the children, composing stories and messages together, demonstrating how writing works, how text operates, and offering opportunities for attending to words and letters.

4. Guided Reading

The teacher mentors a child or a small group through the reading of a selection, drawing them into an exploration of the context, the content, and the words.

5. Independent Reading

Children select books to read individually, or with a partner, from the classroom collection, learning how to read independently as a member of a reading community.

6. Retelling Activities

Retelling is a simple comprehension strategy that can uncover a child's assumptions and understandings, and lead to further reading and responding activities.

7. Literature Circles

After reading a text together, children take part in discussion groups where they experience meaningful literary conversations.

8. Predicting Activities

Before the book is read, children gather their personal experiences and predictions as resources for preparing to read.

9. Questions That Matter

Guiding questions, open – ended questions, children's questions, group puzzlements – all are stimuli for discussion and response activities.

10. Cloze Procedures

Attempting to complete the omitted words in a passage of text reveals comprehension and demonstrates the strategies the reader is using.

11. Response Journals

Children record private thoughts about the text, and sometimes share excerpts with the teacher or trusted others; sometimes the teacher writes back creating a dialogue.

12. Oral Reading Techniques

The children read aloud the text, the dialogue, or excerpts to the teacher or a partner, or share favorite bits with a group. The class can read chorally from shared texts.

13. Charts and Diagrams

The children represent concepts from the text in graphic form, clarifying the story as they work through their ideas and those of the author.

14. Drama and Reading

The children read the text aloud for real audiences who listen to dramatized presentations, to Readers Theatre, or who join in the reading experience.

15. Readers as Writers

Writers who act as readers notice how they construct their own writing. They are learning from the inside out how print holds ideas.

16. Word Power

The teacher creates opportunities for the children to focus on letters, letter clusters, and words in all of the language events as well as designing occasions where children attend to the elements of print (e.g., word walls, language centres, word of the day).

17. Word Play as Literacy

Games, both with paper and pencil and commercial board games, add to the power of print in a collaborative and fun context.

18. Teacher Demonstrations and Mini-Lessons

The teacher presents short, specific sessions on a topic drawn from the children's work, or that have been prepared in order to assist the children in their reading or writing (e.g., how to write a letter to an author, how capitals and periods can help us read and write for understanding).

Part II: Techniques and Strategies

8: Reading Environmental Print

Most children begin to note how print works as toddlers and preschoolers. They become fascinated by print and come to know that it carries meaning. They may recognize:
• words on signs and labels,
• names of fast-food restaurants and brand names,
• their own names,
• words related to dates and themes.

They may be able to print some or all of their name, retell stories, and engage in pretend writing. Some, particularly those whose parents read to them regularly, can locate words in a favorite book. All of these activities lay the groundwork for literacy development.

These early experiences are based on repeated exposure to print, with opportunities to discuss words that they see and hear. The more opportunities children have to experience books, the greater the advantage they will have when they start school. It is this reality that makes it crucial that parents be aware of the role they can play in their child's early literacy development.

At school, young children need plenty of opportunities to explore books, read, discuss, and respond to them. This is particularly true of children whose literacy knowledge stems only from school activities. We need to recognize the needs of all children and supply them with experiences that will help them to develop their literacy abilities. Close observation will inform us of the effectiveness of each child's program and we can modify it accordingly. What we must impart to all children is the sense that they are meaning makers – they read and write and share understandings. Our role is to provide the atmosphere, the activities, the resources, the strategies, the demonstrations that will set them on the path to lifelong literacy – in short, a print environment.

9: Reading Aloud

A story read aloud by a reader is a captivating experience, one that stretches back through time. When children listen to a story read aloud, they are free to see the story in their minds, to imagine the characters alive and in the room with them, to place themselves at the centre of the story.

Reading stories aloud frees us from having to limit book selection to the children's reading ability or previous experiences. We can choose stories that would be too difficult for children to read on their own, or we can read stories that may focus on a culture or topic new to the children. They can experience new worlds, new ways of living, and new experiences. They can travel back in time to be part of an historical story, or they can imagine themselves in some future world as they listen to a science fiction story.

> **Organizing Books**
> • different versions of the same story
> • the same story, with different illustrators
> • works by one author or by one illustrator
> • stories that share the same characters
> • stories that share a similar structure
> • stories that share a similiar theme
> • stories that share the same theme
> • stories from the same culture
> • cultural interpretations of the same story

Reading aloud should not be confined to the primary level. All children can benefit from immersing themselves in a story where they can experience it free of restraints that may accompany other aspects of learning; the read-aloud story allows children to experience literature for its own sake. Children's knowledge of the types of books available – fiction, non-fiction, novel, short story, poem – develops as does their knowledge of how to read these types of books. Their listening vocabulary grows, and they listen to models of effective language structures. They become aware of how plot works and appreciate the author's use of devices to entice the reader to stay with the story. They listen to our voice as we read, and hear phrasing, fluency, and tone.

To bring life to a story we read aloud, we may need to practise it a few times privately. In the beginning, a tape recorder can be valuable as you listen to yourself read aloud and note the tempo with which you speak, the level of conviction you convey, and your ability to use your voice to draw readers into the story. When you're ready, you can introduce the story to children, take a deep breath, and begin!

We may choose a particular story for a read-aloud:
- to reflect a theme the class is exploring,
- to represent an issue with which the children are grappling,
- to reflect a real-world issue we want children to discuss,
- to support the reading that some children are doing independently,
- to illustrate a particular strategy or concept,
- as an outstanding example of literature,
- for the joy of reading.

When children listen to a story read aloud, they are part of a community that values print experiences. They can discuss their feelings and thoughts with their peers, share their predictions, and contrast the story with others they know. The following list of tips may help you build your read-aloud program.
- We need to begin reading to children as soon as possible: songs, tales, nursery rhymes, stories filled with language play.
- We need to reread books with predictable patterns –words, rhymes, sentence structures –so that children begin to internalize the embedded structures and words.
- When rereading a familiar text, pause at key words and encourage children to join in.
- We can read to the children as often as possible, varying the length and type of selection, giving them embedded structures and words.
- Give the title and the name of the author and illustrator when you are sharing a book, and discuss the cover art and blurb on the back with them.
- Choose books above the children's developmental and reading levels, so that you are providing them with ideas, language, and structures they will meet later in their reading.

- You can read picture books to a range of ages if you select carefully and connect the book to the children's lives. Novels, then, should be read to older children, including, of course, bits and pieces that can motivate the children to read the book.
- You can shorten passages as you meet them in the story, to strengthen their impact with the listening audience.
- If the chapters are too long to complete in a day, stop at an exciting spot in a chapter book, so that children are anticipating your reading next time.
- Try to allow time for class discussion after the reading, or encourage written or artistic responses.
- Use plenty of expression when reading, changing your tone of voice to fit the dialogue, adjusting your pace as necessary.
- Many readers read too quickly. You should read slowly enough that each child has time to build mental pictures of the images in the story.
- You should preview the book by reading it beforehand so that you can identify bits you may wish to skip, or shorten.
- You could record books the class has listened to on a wall chart, or in a class book.
- You can have older children reading to and with younger children.
- You can always abandon a book if you have given it a fair chance, and the children find it unsuitable.
- Remember to answer children's questions patiently and with an understanding of who they are. Then you can resume reading to them.

Storytelling

If reading aloud can be thought of as a performance, storytelling can be thought of as taking the performance one step further. It may be a daunting prospect to tell a story without the aid of a text, but we need to consider that children and adults alike tell stories all of the time. When we relate the incidents of a horrific camping experience, we are telling a story. Our daily narratives – what happened on the way to work, what we did on the weekend – are all forms of storytelling.

Storytelling gives children another way to appreciate story. When we tell a story, we can repeat language for effect, we can use literary devices like alliteration, and we can use our voices as instruments to create moods. A well-told story can create a sense of magic in the classroom as children are transported to other lives and other worlds, strictly through the use of the voice.

Just as we can read any form of story aloud, so too can we use any form of story for a storytelling experience – novels, short stories, poems, myths, fairy tales and folktales, our own stories.

Ways to Read Aloud or Tell a Story

1. Read or tell the story in one sitting. Children can choose to discuss the book or think about it on their own.
2. Spread the reading or retelling over several days. Children can predict events at the end of each session, then check their attempts the next day.
3. Invite a guest to tell a story as a surprise for the children.
4. Children can help you to prepare a dramatic retelling. Groups of children can take turns reading aloud a story with you to the rest of the class. They will need a practice session before reading aloud to the class.
5. Children can sign up for times to share a poem with the class, using a text for reference or reciting the poem from memory.
6. Create a combination of read-aloud and told stories, poems, and texts that explore a particular theme as a special event.

10: Shared Reading

In a shared reading experience, the class gathers first to observe and listen to the text, and then to read the same text together. The primary goal of a shared reading experience is to enjoy the reading of the selection and to participate as a member of a literate community. In such an environment, with the support of their peers and teacher, children can read texts that are more challenging than those they might read alone. The experience frees readers who experience difficulties as their problems are less noticeable in a group reading.

Our role includes providing a supportive environment in which children can take chances with their learning; giving input when necessary;

pointing to each word as it is said; focusing children's attention on aspects of the text, such as particular rhyming words; asking children to make predictions; and encouraging discussions at the end of the reading.

Shared reading, using predictable books, helps emerging readers to see the reading process at work and serves as a powerful force in motivating children to learn to read. Success with patterned stories means that some children have experienced what is probably their first reading success and we hope they will be motivated to read more. For those children who have had plenty of experience with patterned books, we can use assisted reading to help them begin to read stories that are less predictable.

Shared reading contributes to the children's knowledge of words, language conventions, and story structures. We can draw their attention to aspects of each of these topics (e.g., new words, the function of punctuation in a sentence, structures particular to a genre) and discuss them after the reading has ended. While patterned books are the most commonly read text in shared reading, you can also use songs, rhymes, poetry, folktales, fairy tales, myths, short stories, and extracts of content texts.

Like reading aloud, shared reading experiences tend to be most popular in primary grades, but they can occur at any grade level. The subject matter of many big books can be quite sophisticated so that older children can read them and then take part in subsequent activities. Shared reading is very effective with ESL readers – they can take chances in their reading without the worry and embarrassment of being wrong. Regardless of the material read or the age of the reader, all readers need to be able to see the text that is being read. For this reason, big books are a popular choice of texts, but texts can be written on chart paper or on overhead transparencies. Pointers can be used as a reinforcement for directionality and to match words on a one-to-one basis.

11: Shared Writing

Shared writing helps young children to develop their writing voice. With our help, they can produce written texts that reflect their thoughts. They see that writing can be used for different purposes and in all subject areas. Children can read basic texts; with our help, they can also write them.

Shared writing provides us with a chance to show children how words work. As we fill in missing letters in a word, or supply a simple word, we can say the word slowly so that children come to understand that a particular letter or group of letters makes a particular sound. When we read a piece aloud, children understand that the written symbols translate into words they know.

The subject of the writing experience can range from building a list and labelling objects through creating a group story or developing an original story. Each time a word is added to the text, the group rereads the text. The pen can be passed among the children, as everyone takes turns to print missing letters and words. As children's writing progresses, they can use word walls and word banks as references. Our role is lessened; we may interject to help children focus on challenging words or concepts, but we leave the children to write the text.

12: Building Word Power

Developing a knowledge of sound-symbol relationships does not require the use of decontextualized drills. Instead, children can take part in actually processing words in word games, matching activities, charting patterns and word families, discussing with peers interesting words they've discovered, and strategies they use to uncover the meaning of new words. Through this work, we can help children learn about patterns, word families, root words, silent letters, and irregular words. As well, we can't overlook the importance of writing: when children have opportunities to write, they can use words they've learned, consolidating their learning of sound-letter correspondences, and furthering their use of all cueing systems.

Shared reading times provide a natural opportunity for exploring sound-letter relationships, including onsets and rimes. Together, we can read children's favorite poems and ask them to find rhyming words and particular sounds. Poems that use alliteration lend themselves to discussions of onsets. Children can work together to produce charts that list onsets and rimes.

As you read aloud to children, you can model strategies (including self-correction strategies) that fluent readers use when they meet a new word – rereading a sentence to confirm the meaning of a new word, asking if the word sounds right and if it makes sense, and using familiar letter clusters to break the word down in order to discover its sounds.

Similarly, shared writing helps children to see that the same words and letter patterns are found in many types of writing – they can use words in a story you have written together in their own independent writing. To help them understand the concept, you can examine a piece of shared writing and ask them to identify high-frequency words in the piece as well as the repeating patterns.

What We Need to Do

1. To begin, we must determine what children already know.
2. We need to focus children's attention on both sound cues and cues they can take from letter sequences.
3. Before, during, and after reading, we can ask them to look at letters, letter patterns, letter clusters, and parts of words, to explore sound-letter relationships.
4. We need to choose texts that provide ample opportunity for examining and analyzing words.
5. Within these texts, we need to highlight examples that lend themselves to word analysis.
6. We need to present words in context so that the focus of children's learning is always on making meaning in text.
7. We can present phonic instruction through the use of words from real texts, including songs, shared reading stories, and word games.
8. We need to share with children, through demonstrations and conferences, that the goal of phonics is to help them learn about words, and by extension, more about reading and writing. What we draw attention to in focusing on a phonics concept must then be applied in a reading context.

13: Increasing Phonemic Awareness

Many children find phonemic awareness (hearing the different sounds in a word) more difficult than phonic awareness (matching print to sounds). Barring physical challenges that limit auditory discrimination, we can help children to become aware of phonemics through shared reading experiences, including reading nursery rhymes and pattern books that contain simple pattern structures and texts that support sound-letter awareness. In addition, we can explore with children pairs of words that share the same sound, and then extend the activity to have them name similar pairs of words. Having children name sounds that are the same focuses their attention on sound units within a word. Rhymes, of course, share similar sounds – children can name rhyming words and make up nonsense rhymes containing one or more pairs of rhyming words.

For those children having great difficulty in recognizing sound differentiations, we can continue to encourage them to increase their sight word vocabulary and their use of semantic and syntactic cueing systems.

Alphabetic Activities

1. Make class alphabet books on a topic the class is exploring or that they are interested in. Children can write and illustrate an alliterative poem for each letter.
2. Make sets of cards that children can match (e.g., word pairs like apple and ant, children's names, initial consonants, digraphs in initial and final positions).
3. Play "I Spy" using initial letters, sounds, and so on.
4. Play changing word games in a specified number of moves (e.g., cat to dog in four words – cat, cot, dot, dog).
5. Make word stairs where the first word in a letter is the same as the last letter that preceded it (words are written like stairs).

    b i g
       o f
         u
          n e a t

6. Make word chains where the first word in a letter is the same as the last letter that preceded it (children circle the matching letters).

    fish have ear red

7. Make a dictionary of fascinating words. Together, write a definition of each, asking the children to spell each word as you write it.
8. Make class displays of objects whose names contain a sound (e.g., long o – notebook, coat).
9. Alphabet centres should include a variety of writing instruments, including a computer if possible, pencils, pens, magnetic letters, and alphabet books. At the centre, children can experiment with writing. They can trace letters, draw letters as art, make rhyming word cards, and construct words with the magnetic letters... As children's knowledge of the alphabet builds, so does their awareness of corresponding sounds.

Encouraging an Awareness of Onset and Rime

Onset refers to consonants that precede the first vowel in single-syllable words, while rime refers to the letters that follow the first vowel. In the word **cat**, for example, the letter **c** is the onset; the letters **at** are the rime. While we all know that sound patterns in English can be inconsistent, there are some common patterns in the language. Knowledge of rimes, particularly at the early grades, can help children read and reinforces the importance of word knowledge – parts (e.g., digraphs, blends, vowel sounds), role (e.g., noun, verb), and meaning – in becoming a fluent reader and writer.

Most children recognize onsets and rimes more readily than they do individual letters. When we encourage children to explore these linguistic units, we are asking them to move beyond analyzing individual letters. Analysis of larger chunks of information (letters) is the next step in word analysis and what fluent readers use.

Nursery rhymes are natural tools to use when beginning the study of onsets and rimes. What children will notice initially is the rime. By focusing their attention on these patterns, we can begin to direct children to specific sound relationships. When children, particularly young children, are encouraged to write, they extend their knowledge of phonological awareness – they see the written symbols that represent the sounds they hear.

Children typically recognize words that share a common sound in the initial position rather than in the final position. Exploration of onsets and rimes can take place throughout the day. Children can make rhyming word pairs by underlining letters that rhyme and circling letters that are different; they can chart words that contain the same onset/rime and post them in the class; and they can play games where they make up new words that share the same rime.

Examples of Onsets

ch- sh- ph- th- wh- gh- wr- sc- pn- kn- gn- ps- br- cr- dr- fr- gr- pr- tr- bl- cl- fl- gl- pl- sl- sw- tw- sc- scr- sk- sm- sn- sp- spr- squ- st- str- thr- chr- shr-

Examples of Rimes

-ab -ace -ack -act -ad -ade -ag -age -aid -ail -ain -aint -air -ake -ale -alk -all -am -ame -amp -an -ance -and -ang -ank -ap -ape -ar -are -ark -art -ase -ash -ast -at -ate -ave -aw -ay -each -ead -eak -eal -ean -ear -eat -ed -edge -eed -eek -een -eep -eet -ell -en -ench -end -ent -est -et -ew -ice -ick -id -ide -ied -ies -ift -ig -ight -ike -ill -ime -imp -in -ind -ine -ing -ink -int -ip -ipe -ish -it -ite -oat -ob -ock -og -oke -old -oll -one -ook -oop -op -ope -ore -or -orn -ose -ot -ote -ouch -ough -ought -ounce -ound -out -ow -own -ub -uck -udge -ug -um -ume -ump -un -ung -unk -unt -ush

14: Developing Phonics Strategies

The following activities ask children to focus on letters and groups of letters, the sounds they represent, and how they combine to form words. Children can work on their own, with a partner, or as part of a group.

1. Filling in the Blank

Record a sentence from a children's book on a letter-sized sheet of paper. Hold the sentence up and ask the children to read it aloud. Then cut the sentence so that each word is on a separate piece of paper. One child can be "it." His or her task is to take one word from the sentence and, while the rest of the children turn their backs and close their eyes, hide the word in the room. When the child has hidden the word, ask the other children to turn, open their eyes, and find the hidden word. When a child finds the word, she or he replaces it in the sentence and the class reads it aloud again. The "finder" now becomes "it," and repeats the activity.

2. Names and Other Concrete Words

Print each child's name on a card, laminate it, and put it in a box. Draw one card each day. The child whose name is drawn becomes "premier." The rest of the children can ask the premier questions about his or her life, family, pets, and so on. When finished, ask the children to watch as you print the premier's name on the board and show capital and small letters. Together, chant the letters as you spell the name. Cut up the name so that each letter is on a separate piece of paper. Children work to reorder the letters to spell the premier's name correctly, chanting the letters. Continue the activity the next day with a new premier. As the premiers' list grows, point out similarities and differences in names, number of letters, first syllables, hard and soft letters (e.g., Cynthia, Connie), and rhyming words. As a class activity, children can create bar graphs of the letters in first and last names, and make up riddles using clues in the children's names.

3. Letter Actions
Laminate cards with a letter on one side and an action on the other (e.g., bounce, dance, gallop, hop, jump, kick, laugh, march, sit, talk, vacuum, walk, yawn, paint). Link the actions with letters and practise them until the children are proficient. Ask a child to come up and pick a letter. She or he shows it to the rest of the children who do the action associated with the letter. Continue the activity until children are better acquainted with the game, then pass out a card to each child. Children take turns showing the action while others try to guess the letter.

4. Count Words
Give each child ten counters. Ask the children to place a counter on their table or desk for each word that you say in a sentence. Begin with short sentences that contain simple words before making the activity more complex by including more words, and words that are more difficult.

5. Clap Syllables
Have the children form a circle. Ask one child to step forward and clap the beats (syllables) in his or her name. Model the activity several times before asking the children to join you. Begin with names that have one syllable, building up to names that have two syllables, then three syllables. Extend the activity by asking children to clap the beats in the names of objects in the room. Can they point to an object and tell you the number of beats in its name? When finished, write examples of single-syllable and multisyllable objects. Clap the beats in each word and discuss with the children the fact that longer words usually have more beats than shorter words.

6. Nursery Rhymes
Once children are familiar with a few nursery rhymes, break the class into two groups. The first group can start a rhyme, but leaves out the last word; the second group says the word to fill in the blank. Other activities include:
- making up new verses to rhymes, using the names of children in the class,
- choral reading rhyming books,
- identifying words from rhymes that sound the same and writing them on the board.

7. Little Words
Tongue twisters are a fun way to review consonants. Find one or two simple twisters and repeat them with the children until they can say them on their own. Make a poster of the tongue twisters, underlining the first letter of each word. Add a new poster for each tongue twister you introduce, and encourage children to decorate them.

8. Cross-Checking Meaning and Content
Write a sentence on an overhead, preferably one about a child in the class and which ends in the child's name. Cover the final word so children cannot see it. Display the sentence, and ask the children to work together to guess the word, giving them clues by showing the first letter, second letter, and so on.

9. Word Families
Begin by discussing with the children the concept that word families contain words that have the same vowel ending and rhyme. On a piece of chart paper, write "ball" on one side; "sit" on the other. Children record the words in the same manner on a piece of paper. Next, write "wall" under "ball"; "hit" under "sit." Children repeat and chant the words. Ask them to give rhyming words and record them in the appropriate column. Children can chant the words in each list.

10. Reconstructing Text
Cut apart or rearrange the text of a story or selection and ask the children to arrange the words to reconstruct its meaning. Pocket charts, magnetic boards, charts, and computers can make the reconfiguring process easier. The children can sequence pictures, pages, lines, episodes, events, sentences, words, and paragraphs. From folders and envelopes they can sort and order statements, titles, words, webs, charts, books, themes, and nouns and verbs.

15: Constructing Words

To introduce this concept, you can write individual letters of a word on separate cards (uppercase on one side, lowercase on the other) in scrambled order. The children make as many little and big words as possible before creating one word that contains all of the letters.

Children, working collectively, can make words, as well as engage in a number of activities, including constructing sentences, exploring sound-letter relationships and letter-vowel-consonant identification, practising capitalization, and transposing letters. Repetition, chanting, rhyming, placing, and writing are effective, fun ways to reinforce learning. Games progress from simple one-letter identification to four and more letters until children create the final word employing all letters (with clues given by you). The words often come from stories children are reading as part of a shared reading experience.

Activities that help children look for patterns in words means that, as emerging readers and writers, they will be increasingly able to recognize familiar words. Children in higher primary and junior grades can make larger words, demonstrating increased reading and writing fluency. In addition to a class pocket wall chart containing letter sets and word combinations, an overhead projector is an effective way to manipulate letters and demonstrate patterns.

Making Word Lists

Children can list words in a variety of ways according to any number of attributes on word walls, charts, or in their notebooks:
- share the same letters,
- begin/end with the same letter,
- rhyme,
- have the same vowel sound,
- describe the same theme or topic,
- have the same number of syllables,
- contain two root words,
- share a pattern (consonant or vowel) in the initial, medial, or final position,
- contain smaller words in order,
- contain silent letters,
- share the same root,
- contain letters that can make other words (sit, its),
- begin or end with the same sound, but don't contain the same letters.

Making Analogies

One of the strongest strategies we can teach children is to draw analogies between concepts they know and concepts they are learning. This is particularly useful in recognizing and constructing, where children sometimes forget existing word knowledge when faced with what appears to be, on the surface at least, a difficult word. By making analogies, children can develop confidence in using what they know to learn new things.

English contains a number of patterns that can be used to decode a word. This knowledge helps emerging readers to predict or recognize a word, and confirms their prediction and understanding. A part of children's growing understanding of reading is their ability to recognize these common letter patterns. As they read, they begin to change their focus from individual letters to the largest cluster of letters in a word. They match the letters to the sound, read other letters in the word, and consider if the word makes sense.

As children's vocabulary grows, so too does their ability to make analogies between learned and new words, helping them to analyze and understand a bank of new words.

Meeting an Unfamiliar Word
1. Say the word slowly. Listen to each sound you hear.
2. What other word contains that sound? Do you know how to say/spell that word?
3. Does the word make sense?
4. Does it sound right?
5. Reread the sentence to check the word's meaning.
6. Do you know other words that contain the same letters?
7. What does the picture tell you?
8. Scan the text for material that might help you understand the word.
9. What is the first letter of the word? What sound does it make? Does this match the word you're thinking of?
10. When you meet a new word, try to figure out its meaning from the words around it. For extra help, look at letter patterns and letters in the words.

16: Building a Sight Word Base

To read effectively, a reader has to recognize words quickly, accurately, and easily. Readers translate written symbols that are grouped into words into their oral representation of those words, hearing them inside the head during silent reading. In order to focus on making meaning, the reader has to become efficient at word recognition, with as little effort as possible.

By the time most children arrive at school they will have some sight-word knowledge, including environmental print (e.g., fast-food signs) and some words in stories that have been read aloud to them. They will usually attach meaning to words, but often not to single letters (except those in their name). Given this fact, presenting letters will have little meaning. Instead, we need to present whole words to children as they begin to read. It is only after children recognize a number of words by sight that we can introduce the concept of phonics cues.

Sight words are those words that a reader recognizes automatically. These words can be frequent words (e.g., the, and, a, then), as well as words that do not follow a set pattern and must be recognized using other techniques. Most of the sight words that we learn to recognize almost subconsciously are learned through reading, where the context helps the reader to make sense of a

word, if she or he is involved in real reading and word construction activities. Teaching sight words requires careful attention. Some readers need to learn to deal with the nature of how words work in the following ways:

- Children need to play with words. Through exploring, constructing, observing specific techniques, and talking about words, they begin to develop an awareness of how words work.
- By seeing difficult or unfamiliar words in a variety of texts, children apply their knowledge of word decoding to make meaning with unknown words. The more children read, the more familiar the words become, and their subsequent recognition of those words becomes more efficient. They begin to see themselves as effective readers.
- Children can use texts that are memorable, such as rhymes and rhythms, predictable patterns, and series like *George and Martha* by James Marshall where the same words are repeated, as well as reading their own compositions and teacher-generated texts that highlight or repeat core words.
- Selecting a text to read in which the children know most of the words allows them to focus on making sense of the text.
- Children need to develop a sense of ownership for the words they are learning to recognize, to retain words that are meaningful to them, and to use elements of known words.
- Children can increase their word power by using words in the context of meaningful reading and writing.
- Children gain new oral vocabulary from their experiences with language used in context for real reasons – books, television, games, talking with friends, and listening to stories.
- Knowledge of sight words or familiar vocabulary is necessary to make sense of a particular piece of text. When there are too many unfamiliar words to decode, a child loses control over the context. Since sight words are necessary for "progress in reading," these strategies are vital for developing readers.
- Children gain new print words through extensive reading and follow-up discussion to ensure that the words become integrated into their personal discourse. Teaching lists of new words out of context has little potential for increasing vocabulary.

- In order for a word to enter a child's personal vocabulary, she or he needs to generalize its meaning and apply it to a new authentic context.
- Dictionaries help children only if they understand concepts related to the word.
- Children will choose from their reading those words they make part of their own vocabulary.
- Children can learn several sight words at the beginning of their first book. This gives them a feeling of success when they pick up a book and immediately recognize several words.
- Children can often substitute words meaningfully and continue to understand what they are reading. A child may read "the" for "a" and still understand the passage. Later, the word can be revisited.
- Children can return to an unfamiliar word as meaning accrues though their context understanding.
- Children can examine text during a class demonstration and point out words that the author has chosen because of qualities the words possess and predict meanings as they connect new words to their personal, internalized lists.

Not surprisingly, as children engage in activities that promote fluency (e.g., rereading, partner reading, choral reading) they begin to recognize words quickly and accurately. As they are exposed to words and word chunks that appear often in text, they begin to respond automatically. Good readers recognize many words, which helps them to focus on concepts, ideas, and the occasional new word as they read. The larger the sight word vocabulary, the easier the reading experience. Encountering a number of difficult words is frustrating for a developing reader, and extra preparation may be required when materials have specialized or uncommon vocabulary.

A love of reading and a fascination with words, along with activities that cause children to think about and use words in meaningful contexts, will help them to build vocabulary through the years. Fluent reading and writing requires the ability to immediately recognize (and spell) the majority of words needed to make meaning. As well, children require strategies for identifying (or spelling) the occasional unfamiliar or difficult word. High frequency words, or words specific to a curriculum topic, can be displayed in a variety of ways so that

children can refer to them as they read and write.

Developing a Sight Vocabulary

1. Matching Words on a Card
After children have read a story in a reading group, write some high-frequency words on index cards. Children who have difficulty identifying a word can go back to the text, find the page that has that word, and using the story context and pictures, match the word on the index card to the word on the page.

2. Pattern Books
Try using pattern books to build sight vocabulary and fluency. Write sight words on index cards so that children can look at each word and examine its letters. Having children write an innovation on the story pattern is another way of reinforcing vocabulary.

3. In-Pin-Spin
Show children how familiar patterns and little words that they know can be used to figure out new words. Write a word that you think the children will know and use it to guide them in reading the new word.

4. Word Prompts
Emerging readers tend to have a difficult time with words such as "they," "what," and "when," especially if these words are at the beginning of a sentence. For example, the word is "they." You can prompt the child by asking, "What did they do?"

5. Meaning from Context
Have children follow along in their book as you read the text aloud. When you come to a word that you expect them to know, pause and observe if children make connections to other words they know and use the meaning of the story to read the word.

Instant Words

Lists of basic sight words are useful because they tell us which words in our language are used most frequently. One such list is the Dolch list, which contains 220 of the most common words found in print. Devised in 1941 by Edward Dolch, the list remains relevant and compares well to newer lists. In terms of children's vocabulary, it seems that

Dolch's list represents approximately 70 percent of words in first-grade reading texts. The words below are the most common words in the English language, and are listed by frequency. The first 25 words represent a third of all print material while the first 100 represent approximately half of all print material. These lists are not intended to be taught out of context to children, but can be useful in understanding and assessing a child's progress.

You can make your own instant word list by using lists such as those below and from words you observe your children writing frequently.

The First Hundred Instant Word

1-25 Words	26-50 Words	51-75 Words	76-100 Words
the	or	will	number
of	one	up	no
and	had	other	way
a	by	about	could
to	word	out	people
in	but	many	my
is	not	then	than
you	what	them	first
that	all	these	water
it	were	so	been
he	wee	some	call
was	when	her	who
for	your	would	oil
on	can	make	its
are	said	like	now
as	there	him	find
with	use	into	long
his	an	time	down
they	each	has	day
I	which	look	did
at	she	two	get
be	do	more	come
this	how	write	made
have	their	go	may
from	if	see	part

Common suffixes: -s, -ing, -ed, -er; -ly, -est

100-200

101-125 Words	126-150 Words	151-175 Words	176-200 Words
over	say	set	try
new	great	put	kind
sound	where	end	hand
take	help	does	picture
only	through	another	again
little	much	well	change
work	before	large	off
know	line	must	play
place	right	big	spell
year	too	even	air
live	mean	suck	away
me	old	because	animal
back	any	turn	house
give	same	here	point
most	tell	why	page
very	boy	ask	letter
after	follow	went	mother
thing	came	men	answer
our	want	read	found
just	show	need	study
name	also	land	still
good	around	different	learn
sentence	form	home	should
man	three	us	Canada
think	small	move	world

Common suffixes: -s, -ing, -ed, -er; -ly, -est

17: Connecting Spelling and Phonics

In the same way that children can use cues to make meaning, they can also use strategies to help them spell words. Strategies like "Say It Slowly" help children to focus on sounds in a word. Mini-conferences in these strategies can help children to see how linking existing knowledge to new knowledge can also help them to spell. The degree to which you will incorporate spelling instruction will no doubt depend to a large extent on the nature of the child's spelling ability. Writing samples can indicate the source of the child's spelling; a program that looks at both composition and transaction will need to be put in place.

Children need to have ready access to a range of spelling resources, including dictionaries, computer software programs that feature a spelling and thesaurus feature, word walls, and pattern charts. Word knowledge can be a dynamic part of the curriculum that crosses subject borders. To increase children's knowledge of word patterns, we can draw their attention to relevant words throughout the day. Children can take part in a number of activities on their own, with a partner, or as part of a small group. While spelling programs vary greatly from classroom to classroom, there are some activities you can put into place to further children's spelling growth:

- highlighting patterns,
- listing the longest word (most interesting word, and so on) they've met in reading and writing,
- collecting homophones, homonyms, and homographs,
- playing Concentration (matching pairs of words with common features), as well as commercial games like Scrabble®,
- discussing strange spellings of words, including silent letter patterns and English/American variations,
- discussing logical spellings, such as those containing roots from other languages,
- completing word searches,
- sharing ways a sound can be spelled (e.g., patterns that make the long **a** sound),
- sharing a weekly spelling strategy,
- describing the spelling strategy they find most effective,
- making charts of words that share a pattern, including onsets and rimes, blends, digraphs, and silent letters,
- working with a partner to edit pieces for spelling mistakes,
- exploring word etymologies,
- exploring word families (e.g., plays, played, player, playing),
- reviewing spelling progress and planning new directions for their learning.

Word Banks

Word banks give children ownership and investment in the words they learn, increasing their interest and enthusiasm for reading. Children choose key words from their reading, based on a quality (e.g., sound, length), record the words on index cards, and file them in a personal word bank. Because the children own their banks, they recognize the words more easily. You may also add complementary words to the bank to emphasize concepts (e.g., sound-letter relationships), but it is the children who ultimately control their bank and the words in it.

Each child may have two word banks or use color-coded cards – one for words that are being learned and one for recognized words. Words can be used in a number of ways: practised, matched, used in posters, made into cartoon captions, discussed, sorted, played with, cut and pasted, expanded, used to generate rhyming words, phrases, or sentences, shared, and traded. Through the use of word banks, meaning is made as children recognize words effortlessly and use them in both contextualized and decontextualized settings. The growing number of recognized words (50 to 150) enables children to read independently texts of increased complexity, as well as to write their own stories with confidence.

Word Walls

A word wall, a visual display of words children have learned, acts as an immediate, accessible class dictionary and aids in the assimilation of high-frequency words. Word walls reflect children's growing body of word knowledge. They can use the word walls as a reference when they read and write, using their existing knowledge of words to extend their learning. Word walls should always be used to associate meaning and practice activities: frequently used words should ultimately be automatic, and not phonetically spelled, in order that children can spend their time and energy decoding and understanding less frequently used words. Five words per week can be added to a classroom word wall, usually all on Monday, so that the wall will comprise 200 to 220 words by the end of the year. Words can be displayed alone, with a picture-sentence clue, or with a picture-sentence-poster displayed in the room.

Words selected for a wall are those children commonly misspell, confuse with other words, or need in their reading and writing. Word walls, which are useful from grades 1 to 5 and higher, are arranged alphabetically on different colored pieces of construction paper. Children can read and write the words each day through clapping, dancing, rhyming, and spelling activities. Other word wall activities include: adding endings (e.g., "s," "ing," "ed") to words; handwriting; making sentences using the first letter; making sentences from wall words; mind reading, in which you think of a word and then give five clues to guess the word; ruler tapping in which you call out a word and then tap out some of the letters without saying them or finishing the word – the children finish spelling the word aloud; and sorting words based on features (e.g., words that start with "t," words that end with "b"). Word walls for older children can include words related to current events or topics they are studying in other courses. In this context, word walls can resemble webs as words relating to shared topics are linked.

Classification Suggestions for Word Walls
- double letters (e.g., daddy, mommy)
- letter clusters (e.g., tion, ish)
- compound words (e.g., goldfish, housecoat)
- unusual letter clusters (e.g., aardvark, vacuum)
- prefixes (e.g., in-, de-)
- suffixes (e.g., -tion)
- root words
- two-, three-, eight-, and twelve-letter words
- silent letters (e.g., ghost, knock)
- rhyming words (e.g., hear, fear, near)
- homophones
- plurals – regular and irregular
- contractions
- abbreviations
- synonyms
- functions
- joining words (e.g., and, but, however)
- alphabetical order

Dictionaries

Dictionaries are only relevant when children understand the concept of alphabetical order and the concept of a dictionary. Once children understand these concepts, they should have access to a variety of writing tools, including picture dictionaries, regular dictionaries, and thesauri. If possible, work with children on the computer to illustrate the spelling and thesaurus sections on most word processing programs.

Based on their work on alphabet books, children can extend this concept to include the creation of personal dictionaries. These dictionaries can comprise regular words they meet in their reading, or they can focus on a particular topic of interest. Discuss in mini-conferences or small-group discussions definitions and how they can vary somewhat from dictionary to dictionary. Children can discuss with peers their progress, as well as some of the words they have included in their dictionary.

Activities

1. A Dictionary for This Century
Ask the children to make a dictionary that contains only words that have developed since the end of the last century. Many of these words describe technological discoveries. Can they determine how the words were formed?

2. A Dictionary for Past Centuries
As children read, ask them to look out for words that are no longer in common use (e.g., thou, thee, doth). They can include a short definition of each word and where they found the word.

3. New Words from Old
Portmanteau words are a combination of two words. One example is *motel*, which is made up of the words *motor* and *hotel*. Ask children to note portmanteau words as they read. When they have recorded five or more words, they can make a quiz for a classmate by illustrating the two original words in each portmanteau word. Classmates look at the illustrations and supply the missing word.

Spelling Activities

1. Spell a Category
Select a theme or subject. Children form groups of four to six players. Each player draws a letter from a bag or box, and spells a word that starts with that letter and fits the theme. One point is awarded for each word that is spelled correctly and fits the theme. The opposing team is awarded a point if a player misspells a word or gives a word that does not fit the theme.

2. Telegrams

In small groups of four, each child takes two turns to say a letter. One group member records the letters that have been called out. The group then organizes the letters so that they represent a coded sentence or message, for example: T S W E D V C A. This could stand for "To Spell Well, Examine Different Vowel and Consonant Arrangements."

3. Word Lists

Children can make lists of words in a variety of ways. As examples, they can classify by:
- letter clusters (ae, oo, ou, ight, tch)
- compound words (rainstorm, snowball)
- portmanteau words
- suffixes and prefixes
- number of letters
- number of syllables
- homographs (words that are spelled the same, but sound different)
- homophones (words that sound the same, but differ in meaning)
- silent letters
- rhyming words
- plurals (ways of forming)
- contractions (can't, shouldn't)
- abbreviations (i.e., e.g., etc.)
- word families
- anagrams (rearranged to make other words (wasp/paws)
- palindromes (same both ways - level, did);
- semordnilap (palindromes backwards yam/ may, evil, live)

4. Rhymes and Songs

Rhymes and songs, in addition to being enjoyable, represent ideal learning opportunities since many contain alliteration, repetition, and rhyming words – the knowledge of which can contribute to spelling development. You can use rhymes and songs from big books, and can write others on chart paper or overheads. As the children sing the rhyme or song, you can use your finger to point to the words.

5. Invented Words

These are common in children's literature and children enjoy creating their own words as well. Discuss with the children how new words are added to our language. Here are some examples;
- acronyms: scuba (self-contained underwater breathing apparatus);

- abbreviations (e.g., ad – advertisement);
- portmanteau words (smoke and fog = smog);
- words that came from names, such as sandwich (named after the fourth Earl of Sandwich, who liked to eat his food between two slices of bread so that he could continue to gamble).

Ask the children to keep lists of new words. For each, they decide what type of word it is (e.g., portmanteau) and, if possible, research and write its history. This type of word study provides children with knowledge about word development and how words are added to our lexicon.

6. Vocabulary-Punctuation

Record the following words on separate pieces of poster board: parentheses, apostrophe, ellipses, question mark, quotation marks, semicolon, dash, comma, colon, period. Record the corresponding punctuation marks on separate pieces of poster board. Children match the two sets of cards.

7. Avoid-a-Word

This game, which works best with two or three players, can be played orally or on paper. The game begins with each player being assigned a random letter. In turn, players must add a letter to their random letter, all the while trying to avoid making a word. (They must have a possible word in mind, and may be challenged to reveal it.) As soon as a word is made, the other player(s) makes one point. Play begins again with the assignment of new random letters.

8. Forbidden Letters

Players, in small groups of two to four, take turns deciding on one letter that cannot be used in answers to any questions. As an example, players decide that the forbidden letter will be "p." Question: What do you like to do at recess? Answer: I like to go out to the yard and enjoy a game of hockey. The player avoids using words like "playground" and "play." When a player uses a forbidden letter, the other player(s) makes one point. Play begins again with the assignment of a new letter.

9. Palindromes

Challenge children to find palindromes (words that read the same way forward and backward). They can find and list palindromes in names (Anna), common words (pop), and even phrases (not Lima Hamilton). Palindromes can also be used in guessing games (e.g., What can you call a young child? (tot).

10. Anagrams and Other Puzzlers

Challenge children to make anagrams by transposing letters in existing words or phrases to make new ones. Beginners could turn "ten" into "net" and "read" into "dear"while more advanced players could turn "kitchen" into "chicken." Similarly, children could look for small words in larger words like "urn" in "turn." A third type of game might consist of unscrambling nonsense words to form words, such as "delcan" to "candle."

11. I Sentence You

This game can be played in small groups of four. Players take turns giving one another short words. The player who receives the word must then make a sentence that uses the letters of the received word in order (e.g., cat = Cathy ate treats). When a player misses or mistakes a letter, other players make a point.

12. Beheadings and Cappings

Beheadings are words that are made by cutting letters from the front of other words (e.g., stowed - towed - owed - wed). In cappings, the action is the opposite because players must add a letter to create new words (e.g., rain, train, strain).

18: Syllabication Rules

Younger children can do some elementary work with syllables by taking part in activities such as clapping out words in rhymes and classifying words according to their number of syllables. Reinforcing the knowledge that words can be divided into smaller units gives children another strategy to call on when spelling.

As children mature, they begin to move away from "pure" spelling activities to focus more on syllables, stress, and etymology. To begin, they work with simple two-syllable words, such as *table* and *window*, where syllable breaks are obvious. As they develop the ability to hear syllables and divide words accordingly, they begin to identify syllables in more complex words and stressed syllables within these words. Underlying all of these activi-

ties is etymology – the origins of words – and how words can be made adding prefixes and suffixes.

To help children develop their word knowledge of syllables and stress, we can share with them the following set of guidelines.

Guidelines for Determining Syllables and Stress

(The following list has been adapted from *Phonics, Too* by Jan Wells and Linda Hart-Hewins.)

1. Each syllable has one vowel.
2. When two vowels surround two consonants divide the word between the two consonants (wil - low).
3. When there is only one consonant between two vowels, break the word after the first vowel (vo - wel). In cases such as this, the first vowel is inevitably long, and the syllable is called open.
4. Divide compound words by breaking the word between the two roots (down - town).
5. When two vowels come together in a two- or more syllable word, break the word between the vowels (cli - ent).
6. In most words that end with a suffix, divide the word between the root and the suffix (ask - ing). The exception is words that end in - ed.
7. Similarly, in words beginning with a prefix, divide the word between the prefix and root (pre - view).
8. In words with patterns such -ble and -tle, break the words before the patterns (ta - ble, sta - ble).
9. If a word contains a digraph that falls after the first vowel in the word, divide the word between the vowel and digraph (go - pher).
10. In most two-syllable words, the stress is usually placed on the first syllable (weath' - er).
11. In words with a suffix, the primary stress is on the root (wait' - er).
12. If these letters and patterns are in the first syllable of word — b-, be-, de-, er-, in-, or- re- — place the stress on the second syllable.
13. If the second syllable of a word contains two vowels together, stress this syllable (be - seech).
14. In two-syllable words with double consonants, divide the word between the consonants and stress the first syllable (run' - ner).
15. In words with the suffixes -ion, -ity, -ic, -ical, -ian, -ious, and -ate, place the primary stress on a preceding syllable (phy - si' - cian). In three-syllable words, it is rare for the primary stress to be placed on the first syllable.

Inflectional Endings (Suffixes)

The first suffix children usually learn is **-s** to make a noun plural (dog - dogs), followed by **-ing** and **-ed** (walking, walked). As their knowledge grows, children learn that adding or changing suffixes can alter the word in a number of ways, including:

- change a verb to a noun (walk - walker);
- change the tense or person of a verb (call - called, she calls - I call);
- change an adjective to a noun (tired - tiredness);
- change the number, case, and gender of nouns (boy - boys, boy - boy's, actor - actress);
- change the degree of adjectives (costly - costlier - costliest).

19: Playing Word Games

Early childhood is full of playful and adventurous experiences with words and language. From babbling sounds and discovering new words to creative imitation and manipulation of language, children enjoy participating in word play. You can use children's inherent love of language to strengthen a language arts program and create a climate in which they enjoy acquiring language competence. Word play extends vocabulary, contributes to an understanding of the technical aspects of language, and gives insight into language complexities – spellings, sounds, rhythms, and incongruities. Using word games in class should be guided by these principles:

- games should help to achieve classroom goals;
- the most important reason for using a game is that it will help children to learn more efficiently;
- games should promote full participation.

1. Jokes, Riddles, and Puns

These are often underused, but they allow children of all ages to use words playfully and enjoyably. Books based on these word plays provide the enjoyable and often brief reading experiences that children crave, and laughter is the payoff for reading. Children often want to share these readings with others.

The irregularities between letters and sounds in English are often confusing. Many jokes and riddles hinge on those irregularities and therefore draw the child into careful reading to discriminate between discrepancies. A number of jokes and riddles involve homographs (words that are spelled the same, but differ in meaning, origin, and often pronunciation). Others involve homophones (words that sound alike but differ in meaning, origin, and sometimes spelling).

2. Tongue Twisters

Tongue twisters actively involve children in playing with words and enjoying the sounds of the language. At the same time, they encourage auditory and visual discrimination and physical articulation. Many tongue twisters involve the children in alliteration, an important poetic device. As an activity, children can hold a tongue-twisting contest. Challenge each child to record and submit a tongue twister (delete repetitions). Volunteers for the contest can pick a number to determine who will go first, second, and so on. The point of the contest is to read the tongue twister correctly in as short a time as possible. It is unlikely that the first round of contestants will need to be timed: if they make it through the tongue twister without making a mistake, they qualify for round two. As the field narrows, a timer may be used to help determine the winner.

3. Rhymes and Verses

Using rhymes and verses in the classroom brings the link between language, poetry, and music to light. Jump rope chants and clapping out the rhythm of words or names in time to the syllables and metre of language provide a natural link to poetry. Songs are one way to bring literacy into the classroom in a fascinating yet meaningful manner. Children enjoy music and singing, and there are many songs that one could teach. Folksongs are especially useful.

4. Crossword Puzzles

Crossword puzzles are available from many sources for a variety of levels. Children enjoy completing crossword puzzles that are challenging but manageable. The words could be listed at the bottom to make the activity easier for children in lower grades. A crossword could also be designed by you or by a group of children in response to a story, novel, or non-fiction book experienced in class. Finally, computer programs allow you to make your own word lists and clues to make cross-word puzzles that children can work on during free time, simplifying the activity a great deal.

5. Board Games
Board games, which involve reading, spelling, and co-operative skills, motivate children and encourage learning. Given their popularity, board games should work well in the classroom. They can also be used in co-operative learning lessons to encourage working in a group with limited activity. You can collect a variety of board games that are popular with children and discuss how each works before making them available to the children.

6. Children's Literature
Last but by no means least, children's literature provides many opportunities for word play, which can lead to children sharing orally with one another and making new reading discoveries. Word play strengthens reading skills, oral language skills, and listening skills, an important component of effective communication. As well, word play can involve children in the writing process in a fun and loosely structured manner that leads to improved writing skills.

7. Character-Title Matching
Give children a series of shapes that represent characters from familiar stories, as well as story titles. Children place the titles in front of them. Under each title, they arrange characters taken from that story.

8. What's the Order?
Cut up a sentence from a text children know well. With a partner, they reorganize the sentence to show its original order. Partners can then challenge each other by recording and cutting sentences from stories or books they have experienced. The partner must try to reorder the sentence correctly.

9. What's Missing?
This activity is similar to What's the Order? but instead of working with words in a sentence, children work with sentences in a passage. As in the previous activity, they can challenge each other using texts both partners have experienced. An alternative is to take one sentence out. Can the partner spot its absence?

10. Mixed-Up Texts
Cut sentences from two texts and mix them together. Ask a child to first sort the sentences according to the text they were taken from, and then arrange them in order. Children can also do this activity with a partner who has experienced the same books and stories.

11. Fishing for Words
Cut fish shapes from a large piece of poster board. Give each child a fish and ask him or her to write a favorite word. When finished, children paste a paper strip to their fish. While they are working, make a fishing pole using a stick (should not have sharp ends), a piece of string, and a magnet. Tie the string securely around the magnet and attach it to the stick. Place the completed cards in a large cardboard box that will serve as a pond. Children can work with a partner to fish. One partner puts the stick into the pond of words and fishes for a word. She or he detaches the word, reads it silently, says it aloud to the partner, and gives a brief definition. If correct, the child fishes for another word. If incorrect, the partner takes his or her turn to fish.

12. Rhymes and Verses (Chants, Cheers, Song)
Teach a song by rote (sing one line, the children echo). Repeat this process until the entire song has been learned. Once the words have been learned by the children, they can be incorporated into language activities. Write the words on the overhead and ask the children to read along while you sing. Leave out certain words of a song, and ask the children to fill in the missing words. Talk about the meaning of the song, where it came from, its cultural background, and when it was written. Geography and some social studies activities can be based on information from or about a song.

20: Deepening and Extending Comprehension

1. Real reading experiences motivate children to explore ideas because what is being read is significant to them, enabling "deep-structure" meaning making to occur.
2. We need to help children reveal their thoughts about what they have read so that they can begin to clarify, modify, revise, and extend their frames of reference.
3. Each child must focus on making meaning for himself or herself in becoming a thoughtful reader. Comprehension is about thinking, connecting, and understanding, and it is affected by personal knowledge and experience, and the reasons and situation for reading a particular text. Proficient readers are aware of the techniques involved in making the most possible meaning with print – questioning, predicting, confirming, revising hypotheses, drawing conclusions, anticipating.
4. Proficient readers take risks. They learn to make educated guesses, predicting what the words in print may mean, rereading for clues that are missing, confirming predictions, and making alternate predictions. By caring about the reactions children have to what they read, we can encourage them to speculate about the text, to think about its meanings, to reread for clarification, and to recognize difficult words through word analysis and context clues.
5. Guided reading, book clubs, literature circles, and discussion groups all increase children's understanding of a text and help them to reflect on its aspects. The discussion component allows children to rethink and extend their understandings.
6. We can encourage children to respond in a variety of modes to revisit what they have read, helping them to think about the text in personal and meaningful ways. These interpretations, whether they be through art, drama, talk, or writing, can be shared, increasing everyone's understanding of how text can be appreciated and valued.
7. We can help children to assess their reading ability by providing them with activities and frameworks that promote sharing and exploration, and that continue the inquiry process.

21: Connecting Thinking and Reading

We need to understand the interconnectedness of thinking and reading and language, so that what we are promoting with children will lead to deeper thought. It may help to keep in mind the various processes involved in reading a passage, remembering that all four are intertwined as the mind works.

1. Literal or Factual Understanding (Textually Explicit)
- responds to "Right There" questions raised in the text
- locates significant and insignificant details
- orders items in sequence
- reads and follows directions
- answers question types such as "true or false"

2. Interpretive or Inferential Understanding (Textually Implicit)
- responds to "Think and Search" questions by deducing answers implied in reading materials
- answers questions by drawing conclusions and making generalizations
- predicts outcomes
- summarizes material read
- senses the author's purpose and mood
- finds the main idea

3. Creative or Applied Understanding (Textually Implicit)
- responds to "On My Own" questions by combining existing knowledge with knowledge gleaned from the text in order to arrive at new knowledge base, including emotional connections
- applies knowledge from reading to storehouse of problem-solving strategies
- completes art activities following reading
- writes creatively (prose and poetry)
- completes content activities following reading
- completes drama and creative activities following reading

4. Critical or Evaluative Understanding (Textually Implicit)
- responds to "Think and Search" questions by evaluating the reading material
- discriminates between real and make-believe (fact and fiction)
- evaluates the accuracy or truthfulness of the reading material
- compares information from several sources
- senses an author's biases, and personal biases
- recognizes propaganda techniques (e.g., testimonials, emotional words)

22: Setting the Stage for Comprehension

There are several factors that can increase a child's comprehension, including prior knowledge of the topic, prior exposure to the author's work, or a personal connection to the topic. If a child is about to read a text but has none of these factors, we can increase his or her chances of success by giving some background knowledge that relates to the text. In addition, we can review aspects of the text, including chapter heads, supportive visual cues, and vocabulary that the text contains. This is not to say that we preteach vocabulary; rather, that we acquaint children with the type of terminology they are about to meet in their reading.

If a group is about to undertake the reading of a text, we can help them conduct a more formal preview, including brainstorming questions based on information from the cover and backcover, predicting events that might occur based on this information, researching the topic by viewing films, listening to stories on the same theme, and inviting guest speakers who have knowledge of the topic to share some of their knowledge with the group.

How to Encourage Prediction

1. Emphasize the importance of predicting by reading/viewing with the children. Discuss the fact that each reader comes to a text with different knowledge and experiences, and thus comprehends it somewhat differently from his or her peers.

2. Invite children to predict a text's vocabulary, language style, structure, and content from its title, cover, table of contents, pictures, photographs, and diagrams.

3. Ask questions of the children, including "What do you know?" "What do you want to find out?" Encourage children to form questions using words such as who, where, when, what, why, and how.

4. Have children consider previous experiences related to what they are about to read. Questions can focus and extend the child's thinking about a particular aspect related to the material at hand. The discussion itself may also generate new questions.

5. Divide a short story into three or four episodes. Title each episode and record it on a separate piece of paper. Copy and attach the three or four pages so that each child or pair of children has a booklet. Ask them to read the title of each episode and draw a picture of what they think it is about. When finished, children can compare and discuss their picture sequences. Read aloud the story to the class. How accurate were children's predictions? Discuss with them how the titles helped/didn't help them to predict.

6. Before reading an unfamiliar non-fiction text, write its title on the board. Ask the children to brainstorm sentences they think would be in the text. (An alternative is to have children brainstorm on their own or in pairs, and record their sentences before a class list is compiled.) As a large group, classify the sentences and display them where all children can see them. During and after reading, they can note how many of their predicted sentences were included in the text. A variation of this activity is to ask children to brainstorm words that will be in the text.

7. Provide pairs of children with a series of pictures, words, sentences, or combinations of these related to, or from, a text. Ask them to determine methods of grouping, classifying, and sequencing the elements. Children can share their work with another pair. Together, the four pool their work and present it to the rest of the class. Make a class list of organizational methods.

8. Before children begin to read a piece of text, ask "What do you already know about this

topic?" Record all responses. After children have finished brainstorming, ask them to categorize or classify the information to give it a logical structure. Each child can then identify what they want to find out by writing one or two sentences. At the end of reading, take a class poll to find the number of facts that were answered by the book.

9. This activity reminds children of what they already know and helps them link this to new information. It also clarifies the purpose of reading. Before reading, ask the children to list all they know about a topic to be studied. After reading, they write all they have learned. Children then find a partner with whom they compare lists, and write questions they still need answered. Together, they research the questions and write a short report that details their findings.

10. This strategy directs children to set a purpose for their reading. Ask them to list all headings and subheadings of a book. With a partner, they brainstorm the contents of each section of the book and select what they think will be included. Each child reads the book and substantiates or revises the predictions. When finished, the children meet with their partners to revise information, record changes, and add other information.

11. Discuss a text to be read by outlining its content and objective. Children establish a purpose for reading the text, for example, reading for enjoyment, skimming for a piece of information, or rereading sections for detail. Encourage children to decide on how they will read each new text.

12. Charts can help children to clarify vocabulary and use context clues to work out word meanings. Each child records new words she or he has met while reading and includes a brief description, based on content. This provides children with practice in paraphrasing, a useful skill in making notes and summarizing. If necessary, model the strategy until children are comfortable recognizing and using context clues.

13. A basic knowledge of text layout can help children to comprehend texts. Consequently, a graphic outline, a diagram of information located in the text, can be used by children as a framework for notetaking or summarizing in-

formation. Ask children to look through a text and list features, in sequence, on the left-hand side of the page (e.g., main heads, subheadings, diagrams, maps). On the right-hand side of the page, they record information in boxes, the size of which corresponds to the importance of the information. To help children, give clues as to how many ideas or points may be included under each heading.

23: Supporting Comprehension During Reading

In the past, we would often introduce a text and follow up with activities, but would leave the children to read the text independently. We now know that some children benefit from interjections that will help them to focus on reading for meaning. For some, the content may be daunting; for others, class noises may interfere with their reading; for others, the period of time may be too long for them to sustain their concentration. We can assist them as they read in a number of ways: asking questions that have them reflect on what they have read this far; asking them to predict events based on what they have read; talking with them about their reading, doing cloze procedures with a few children, or asking them to jot their reactions to their readings in their journal. In this way, children are redirected to focus on the text, and we are provided with some insight into their understanding of the story, as well as concepts and vocabulary that may be troublesome.

24: Extending Comprehension After Reading

Response activities help to confirm for children the purpose of reading – to make meaning. Reflecting, rereading, revisiting, and then responding help children to develop critical thinking skills.

They evaluate what they have read, link it to personal experience and prior knowledge, and compare and contrast the experience to other, similar experiences. We need to encourage children to respond to text in a variety of ways so that they view response activities, not just as an activity to complete after reading, but another way that they can extend their learning.

What we look for in responses to reading are instances where children may challenge previous notions they had about a topic, share new learning with others, discover a new way of viewing a character or an event, see the story in a larger context, and connect what they have read to all aspects of their learning. We need to encourage them in their responses and in their reading, for it is the accumulation of positive, enjoyable reading experiences that will drive them forward to become lifelong learners.

25: Metacomprehension Strategies

Teaching strategies for metacomprehension can help at-risk readers focus on how they are learning to read. The strategies can be assigned according to where they occur in a reading – before the reading, during the reading, or after the reading.

Metacomprehension Strategies

Before Reading
1. Consider prior knowledge of a topic.
2. Look at text clues, including the text's cover, illustration, table of contents, and subheadings.
3. Decide on a method of reading based on information from the text clues.
4. Form questions about the reading, make predictions, and discuss the terminology they may meet while reading.
5. Set a goal for reading.

During the Reading
1. Check predictions and form new predictions.
2. Check unanswered questions and form new questions.
3. Check comprehension by rereading.
4. Link prior knowledge to what they have learned.

5. Reread known words around the unknown word.
6. Look for roots and word endings as a clue.
7. Locate sounds within the word.

After the Reading
1. Check the accuracy of predictions.
2. Consider questions that were answered, and others that were unanswered.
3. Review the main points of the story.
4. Think about the knowledge they have gained from reading and link it to their existing knowledge.

Teaching Strategies for Reading

Perhaps one of the greatest stumbling blocks for children who are considered at risk is that reading appears to be a mystery. We can help children to see that reading is made up of a series of steps and strategies that can be consciously used.

We can model aloud the strategies we use when reading on an incremental basis. As children observe our modelling, we can ask them to apply the strategies to a text we are all reading. It is important that children think about the process and verbalize aloud how they are going to read the text.

As children grow comfortable in using a particular strategy, we can ask them to write about how the strategy works and how it helps their reading. The act of writing can make the strategy concrete for the children and allows them to move forward to include other strategies in their own reading.

Metacomprehension Strategies

1. What Is a Book?
Consider, as a class, what constitutes a book before developing a reference chart of types of books (e.g., narrative, non-fiction, poetry). Give the children opportunities to classify books according to the chart.

2. What's in a Title?
Children can discuss the importance of a book's title. To facilitate this, you can display, compare, and discuss various titles and their effectiveness. Can children identify the importance of an effective title? Can children rely on a title to tell them about a book?

- Children can use the title of a book and its cover to make predictions about the story. Record their predictions on a chart and post it in the class. After reading, children review the accuracy of their predictions.
- Children can read or listen to a non-fiction book, then create a web of information.
- Cover the title of the book. After reading it, each child can decide on what she or he thinks is an appropriate title. The children share their titles with a partner.

3. Modelling Published Books

Children can use published books as a model to create their own book. They can include components, such as a dedication and table of contents, and can organize the content in chapters, and model how authors chunk text.

26: Developing Reading Strategies with Young Readers

When readers develop strategies for understanding text and for monitoring their own reading, they are on their way to becoming fluent, independent readers who can assume control and responsibility for their learning. Along the way, they need secure environments in which they can experience plenty of success in their reading ventures, where they feel safe to experiment and make errors or miscues in their reading. It is through these miscues that children learn to self-correct and self-monitor their reading of a text.

There are three basic understandings that serve as the foundation for our reading programs: readers expect text to make meaning, they want to make meaning with text, and their meaning making is influenced by their previous experience and knowledge.

All readers need our time and attention, but troubled readers in particular benefit from individual attention. We need to encourage these readers to continue their reading of real texts at the same time that we assist them in learning to use the necessary strategies.

These readers need literacy programs that have been modified to reflect their needs. We need to provide them with successful reading opportunities that will contribute to their satisfaction and cause them to want to read more. They need time to think about what they have read, to prepare for a new reading, to wander through libraries, and to develop their personal reading tastes. As children come to see themselves as readers, we can work with them directly and indirectly on a host of reading strategies that will lead to their reading success.

All readers use strategies and processes to help them integrate new information with existing knowledge. In this way, we can call on this integrated knowledge as we apply it, transform it, relate it to other bodies of knowledge, shape it, and use it to communicate.

Strategies and processes are, to a large extent, intangible. Because of this, we can never be certain how children employ them. Instead, we need to watch for evidence of specific strategy use, and the degree of success children meet when using them. One effective method for assessing strategy application is the use of running records. When taken every two to four weeks, they provide us with examples of the process of reading and the application of strategies.

When good readers read aloud fluently, they use phrasing to communicate their meaning. When they read silently, they interpret the text and add it to their knowledge base. Less fluent readers, on the other hand, tend to read at the same speed, no matter what the text, both silently and orally, and use the same phrasing. They may not use all of the syntactic cues a text provides or the many factors that contribute to comprehension (e.g., cues such as sub-headings).

Most children have absorbed the rules of oral language and their knowledge is reflected in their use of both vocabulary and structures in their talk. For this reason, young children can often read texts where the written language is reflective of oral language in both the syntax it uses and vocabulary it includes. In addition to these familiar components, children bring existing knowledge to many of the topics explored in these books. They use their knowledge to anticipate events in the story, as well as how the information will be organized. The ability to process visual cues and use sight vocabulary also contributes to fluent reading, as does the ability to make use of the features of unfamiliar words.

It is important that the books, and the introductions to them, are appropriate to a reader's ability and experience. The texts should be readable and contain plenty of familiar words along with some new words and concepts. Our introductions should enable children to determine the process they will use to read the text as well as introduce a few of the words children will meet in their reading.

While good readers read quickly, they may not always read accurately. Instead, they use particular strategies when they discover through self-monitoring that they have made a reading error. Before they can do this, however, they need to be able to anticipate text, use meaning and syntax cues, and recognize letter clusters – strategies that beginning readers need to focus on in order to make connections between print and their reading abilities.

We need to help young readers develop self-monitoring strategies so that they have on hand strategies such as rereading the text, checking picture cues, and breaking an unfamiliar word into more manageable chunks. As their fluency grows, they begin to do this work silently and their use of strategies starts to reflect their growing reading ability.

With young readers, beginning texts, where the print is heavily supported by pictures, are appropriate vehicles to use to encourage children to self-monitor. They can use both print and visual cues to make sense of the text. Effective emerging readers read for meaning and use the pictures as backup. They notice both aspects as needed. We need to help children learn how to solve words while reading, not only before meeting the text nor just after the text has been completed.

Good readers are those who self-monitor their reading, use all cueing systems simultaneously, compare information using several sources, and confirm their reading using a variety of techniques. They can apply the strategies they have developed to read more challenging texts.

Developing Independent Readers

1. Anticipating Meaning
Children need to understand that the point of reading is meaning making. As readers, we expect text to make sense. When it doesn't, for example, when we encounter difficult words, we use semantic, syntactic, and phonic information to help us understand the word's meaning and pronunciation.

2. Word Solving
When good readers come across a difficult word they may skip over it with a view to revisiting the word later; they may analyze the word for letter-sounds; they may predict a word's meaning based on context and check back by rereading the sentence. These are useful responses to challenging words.

3. Cross-Checking Print Information
Good readers often check information gleaned from one cueing system against information from one or more systems (e.g., using the cue of the s on boys against a picture of a group of boys, or the fact that the unknown word must be a noun). If the two sets of information are congruent, the reader knows she or he is accurate.

4. Review Reading
When children continue reading a selection over several days, a brief review of material they have read is necessary. We can help them to tell the story to the point where the reading ended, and then ask them to continue reading (e.g., writing a short summary that they read aloud, rereading a passage in the text that summarizes recent events, rereading the last page read).

5. Predictions
Each time we read, we predict what will come next, whether it be a content issue or a word. We make these predictions based on semantic, syntactic, and phonics cues, which we sometimes use simultaneously. As our reading grows, so, too, does our ability to anticipate what comes next. We can help children to develop this ability (and prepare for their reading) by discussing a few unfamiliar concepts and words before the reading.

27: Prompts for Assisting a Young Reader

Prompts for Retelling After Reading
- What is the topic of the text?
- What did you think of the text?
- Do you have questions about the text?
- Did you reread parts of the text?
- What did you do to understand difficult parts/words of the text?
- What new words did you learn by reading this text?
- Were you able to predict the meaning of new words in the text?
- How did your past experience with the topic of the text help you to understand this text?
- Would reading more material on this topic help you to better understand the text?
- How do (genre) _____ usually begin? How do they end?
- Do we talk the way the text (novel) is written?
- Show me the book's table of contents and chapter headings.
- Show me the book's index and subheadings.
- Find the page where _____ is described.
- Tell me how I would use the table of contents.
- How do the pictures help you understand this book?
- Can you find the location of the topic or story in an atlas?
- Where else can you find out more about this topic?
- What part of the story did you choose to read? Why?
- Can you tell me what happened in the story to that point?

Prompts for Analyzing Unfamiliar Words While Reading
- Think about what word would make sense.
- How did you know it was that word?
- You stopped for a moment before you corrected yourself. What were you thinking? What did you notice? What information did you use?
- Is there any other way you could have known the word?
- Were you thinking about the story while you looked at that word?
- I noticed that you looked at the picture and used the first sound to read that word. Did you use anything else?
- What else could you do to find out if it's the right word?
- Try sampling a word and then read on to see if another word comes into your head.
- Listen to yourself read as you look at the word. What sounds right and looks right?
- Check to find out if what you read makes sense.
- There was something not quite right on that page. Can you find it? What can you use to fix it?
- Are those the letters you would expect to find here?
- What letter would you expect to see at the beginning of the word? What letter would you expect to see at the end of the word?
- Would _____ make sense?
- Do you think it looks like _____ ?
- Try to sound out the word in chunks. Can you figure out the parts of the word?
- Where have you seen the word before?
- Read it with your finger.
- Does it make sense in the story?
- Skip the word and go on to the end of the sentence. Come back and try again.
- Does the word seem to sound right there?
- Can you read this part again quickly?
- Put the words together so it sounds like someone talking.
- Predict a word. Does it make sense?
- Did you expect to see these letters in the word you predicted?
- Do you know a word that looks like this one? How is it the same? How is it different?
- Look at the picture to help yourself.
- What happened in the story when...?
- It could be _____, but what about _____ ?
- You said _____ . Does that sound right?
- You said _____ . Does that make sense?
- Look at how the word begins.
- Does that sound right to you?
- Start that sentence again.
- Think about a word you know that has the same sound in it.
- Put in a word that makes sense, and go on. Is that right?
- Check that again.
- What do you see here?

- Were you right?
- What did you notice? (after hesitation or stop)?
- Why did you stop reading?
- Can you find what is wrong?
- What's wrong with this? (repeat child's word). Try it again. Does it make sense?
- Do you think that could happen?
- Is there such a word as _____ ? It sounded a little strange to me.
- You read _____ . Is that right?
- Think about the story. What might happen next?
- Read ahead for more clues.
- Let's read it again (or reread it) together.
- What sound does _____ end in? Can you think of a word that rhymes with it?
- If we don't hear the **e** at the end of the word, what vowel sound do you think you will hear in this word?
- If a word has two consonants and one vowel, what vowel sound do you think you will hear in this word?

Prompts for Supporting Self-Corrections
- You read ahead to figure out the meaning of a word.
- You checked that your reading made sense.
- You read the material aloud as if you understood it.
- You checked several ways to make sure you had the right word.
- You're nearly right.
- I liked the way you solved that word.
- You made a mistake. Can you find it?
- When _____ didn't sound right, you went back to fix it.
- I didn't need to help you with that! You did all the work yourself!
- I noticed that you sampled sounds and read on to figure the word (meaning) yourself.
- You reread that part to check that word. Did it work?
- I noticed that you used the information from the story to help you correct the word that didn't make sense there.
- I noticed that you stopped for a moment. Were you thinking about the story when you fixed that part?
- I liked the way you did that. Can you go back and find the difficult part (word)?
- Where was it?

- I noticed that you were thinking about the story as you were reading. Good thinking!
- I noticed that you were looking at the pictures to help you read that word. Good work!
- I noticed that you were listening to yourself read to decide if you were right.
- Great! You looked carefully at the words while you pointed to make sure your voice matched.

Prompts to Help a Child Write an Unfamiliar Word
- Find the word on the word wall.
- Check the book for help
- Find the word in your story.
- Ask a friend for help.
- Think of a word you know like this one.
- Write how you think the word is spelled.
- Use a thesaurus.
- Leave a blank and come back later.
- Check the dictionary.

Supporting Young Readers
1. Encourage children to
   - predict the meaning – they confirm their prediction using visual information from the word,
   - reread a sentence that contains a difficult word – make the sound of the first letter in the word so that children can use a context and a sound cue,
   - think of a word they know that is similar to a word they are having trouble with (e.g., row – blow),
   - look for a smaller word in a larger word – they spell the word they know, then spell the rest of the word,
   - distinguish between two sounds or words before teaching what is different,
   - break down larger chunks of information rather than analyzing a word letter by letter,
   - use their fingers to follow the text,
   - make several checks to confirm their responses.
2. Teach by including plenty of demonstrations throughout the day.
3. Give examples of a concept you are teaching, then provide them with the strategy they need to find further examples.
4. Work with a child on a weak area to master it before introducing another problem to work on.

5. Teach according to the problem (a child who has difficulty sequencing can work on activities that focus on this concept).
6. Encourage all attempts at self-corrections, regardless of their degree of effectiveness.
7. Focus children's attention on self-correcting strategies (e.g., I like the way you reread the sentence to find the meaning of _____).

28: Conducting a Running Record

A running record is a type of miscue analysis and presents a record of a child's reading behavior on a specific text. It was developed by Dame Marie Clay in New Zealand.

The teacher sits beside the child while the child reads the text, so that both the teacher and the child are looking at the same text. The child reads a text that he/she has read before, although on occasion, a new text might be read once or twice as a final assessment of progress. The text should be one that presents some challenges so that the teacher can observe the problem solving strategies the child is using. However, it should not be so difficult that the child cannot continue to read. Children should be reading a text with a high degree of accuracy, a guide being 90%; otherwise, the child cannot put into use the strategies that he/she possesses, resorting to guessing or to sounding words out at the expense of understanding the meaning.

As the child is reading, the teacher observes closely, coding the child's reading attempts on a form, using the symbols that follow. The teacher acts as an observer rather than instructor, recording all of the information as the child reads. If the child cannot continue because of a difficult word, the teacher can tell the child the word, so that the reader can move forward to maintain fluency.

The teacher records each word read accurately by the child with a tick: ✔✔✔✔✔ would indicate the child read 5 words in the line of text accurately. The recording of the checks should match the format of the text being read. Each mismatch can be recorded with a line: ✔✔_____✔✔.
Above the line, the teacher can record the child's reading behavior, and below the line, the teacher can record the text information and any teacher

assistance. For example, ✔✔ t̄ext ✔✔ would indicate the child omitted the third word in the line of text, and that word is written under the line, with a dash above the line representing the omission. In this way, the teacher will have a record of the child's reading strategies by the end of the passage, adding to the information about the child's reading progress.

A Modified Running Record

Words Read Correctly
- marked with a check on the blank form
  ✔✔✔✔✔

Omission
- words are skipped accidentally or deliberately
- write the word above the line
  ✔✔ ___ ✔✔
  text

Addition
- words inserted that are not in the text
- write the word above the line
  ✔✔ added word ✔✔
  ___

Pause
- the child is analyzing each word
- the child has a few strategies to use
  ✔ / ✔ / ✔ / ✔ / ✔

Substitution
- a different word for the one on the page is substituted
- write the attempt above the line
  ✔✔ attempt ✔✔
  text

Repetition
- rereading to promote understanding and to build fluency
- place an R after the word or phrase that was repeated
  ✔✔R✔✔

Reversal
- reverses words out of order
- indicate with an arrow
  ✔✔✔✔✔

Correction
- the error is self-corrected by the reader
- place S C above the line
  ✔✔ SC ✔✔
  text

Word Supplied by Teacher
- intervention by the teacher so that the child can continue to read
- place a T under the line and the word above the line
  ✔✔ text ✔✔
  T

The running record for a page of text with 5 lines of print would look like this:

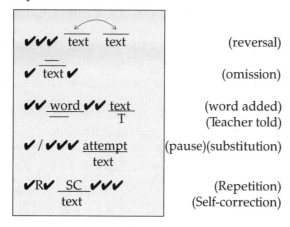

✔✔✔ text ⁀ text	(reversal)
✔ text ✔	(omission)
✔✔ word ✔✔ text / T	(word added) (Teacher told)
✔ / ✔✔✔ attempt / text	(pause)(substitution)
✔R✔ _SC_ ✔✔✔ / text	(Repetition) (Self-correction)

We can share with the child the point of the exercise, since running records are observation tools and not tests. If a child perceives it as a test, she or he may "freeze" and make miscues that do not reflect the child's true reading behaviors and ability.

While the process is time-consuming, it does yield valuable information about a child's reading behaviors and his or her understanding of the reading process. The most common miscues we find in running records are substitutions, omissions, insertions, and reversals. They fall broadly into three categories – graphic change, meaning change, and structure change. Of these three, those mistakes that result in a change of meaning are most serious, since they reflect a lack of understanding of the text on the child's part. If a child makes several graphic or language mistakes, then self-corrects, we can assume that she or he can comfortably read the text. If the child makes mistakes in all three categories, particularly those relating to meaning, and doesn't self-correct, we can determine that the passage is too advanced for the child.

Running records can help us:
- build an accurate reading profile of each child,
- match readers to texts that reflect their ability and interests,
- group young readers for instruction (ability groups for beginning readers for part of the day only),
- offer support for at-risk readers,
- monitor reading growth over time,
- identify the cues, strategies, and information sources the reader uses,

- observe a reader's self-monitoring and correcting strategies,
- become aware of the meaning-making strategies a reader uses,
- observe the fluency of the reading,
- add to our knowledge of how a child is developing as a reader.

Assessing a Running Record
1. Was the text appropriate for the child? Too easy? Too difficult?
2. Did the child read with understanding?
3. What cues did the child use?
4. What strategies did the child exhibit?
5. Did the child self-correct?
6. How has the child's use of cueing systems and strategies changed during the last month?

29: Grouping Children for Reading

The issue of grouping raises some interesting dilemmas. We know as teachers that groups are a necessary component of any classroom – as much as we would like, it is virtually impossible to organize and maintain completely individualized reading programs. As well, peer groups are a strong motivating force in supporting a literate classroom. However, we also know that traditional formal reading groups do not benefit children, particularly those who are experiencing difficulty. We need to devise a way in which the needs of all children are met and their development fostered: we want to protect children from the less-than-beneficial aspects of traditional grouping based strictly on reading level throughout their school years.

The benefits of sound grouping cannot be underestimated. As group members, children develop their skills of communication and co-operation. They can learn from another's experiences, and pool their interpretations of text to increase one another's comprehension. They develop respect for their classmates and their points of view, and they improve problem-solving and decision-making strategies. Also, when children work in co-operative groups we are provided with constructive

46

glimpses into how each child works as part of a group, and the classroom structure enables us to work one-on-one with children who may need assistance with a particular task.

Factors and Benefits of Reading Groups

1. Guided direction in different aspects of print can be implemented.
2. Small groups give children opportunities to re-read sections, noting how print and text work.
3. Children have the opportunity to read a variety of genres and authors that they may not have been exposed to previously.
4. Children's responses can relate directly to the text and can include relevant personal experiences.
5. Children can discuss questions and pool their insights.
6. Children's responses to stories, poems, novels, and reports can include complex discussions of aspects of the material read. This strengthens children's critical thinking skills.
7. Children can share with their group members parts of the book they particularly liked, aspects that puzzled them, and techniques they found particularly effective – book talk in its truest sense.
8. Children can work independently on activities, some where participation is required and others where the child can decide. A scheduling chart may help children organize activities, and a log can keep a child on track.

Types of Groups

In past years, almost all reading groups were based on the children's abilities. Given the detrimental outcomes of such grouping, many of us now choose to form groups based on a variety of factors, and have children meet in groups based on ability only for guided reading activities in the primary grades. In any group, at any level, children should read materials – stories, poems, novels, non-fiction texts – that appeal to their interests and that are suited to their abilities. We can help them by providing a focus for their reading and by helping them relate their reading to their learning and to their lives outside the classroom walls.

Heterogeneous Groups

All children benefit from heterogeneous grouping. Those children who have highly developed abilities can help peers who are less able. In such a situation, both children benefit. For the child receiving the assistance, the benefit is obvious. For the child who is helping, she or he is also learning – to instruct one must evaluate what one knows, organize information, and deliver it in a concise, comprehensive manner. In heterogeneous groups, the likelihood increases that at least one member of the group can contribute his or her experiences to the reading. Heterogeneous grouping supports the belief that classrooms are communities – all members have something to contribute, all are viewed as a part of the greater whole, and all can take part in shared reading, literature circles, and readers' and writers' workshops.

Homogeneous Groups

While there will still be some occasions when homogeneous grouping can benefit children (e.g., when teaching a mini-lesson), there are some negative aspects of such grouping. No matter what a group is called, children in classes where homogeneous grouping is carried out know why each child is assigned to a particular group. We need to look at consequences of fixed, traditional grouping, which include the following aspects.

1. We often set lower standards for children in lower ability groups because we want them to meet with success. However, our goals can be too low. Instead of benefitting the children, we entrench their self-image of unsuccessful readers.
2. Children in these groups often have fewer opportunities to read. When they do read, they tend to spend more time focusing on decoding words than do their counterparts in other groups.
3. Similarly, we expect more behavioral problems from these children than their higher-achieving counterparts. Often, we get what we expect.
4. The tendency is to ask children in low-level groups simple questions that can be answered by a "Yes" or "No" response. In doing this, we do not encourage them to think critically. In addition, such responses are easy to "correct."
5. Once a child is assigned to a low group, she or he tends to stay there throughout their school years.

Guidelines for Grouping

Instituting a series of guidelines will help you to monitor the structure of your groups, the progress of individual children, and the amount of movement between groups.

> 1. Form groups based on reading interests, activities, and topics children want to explore. Consider dividing your class into four large groups on a heterogeneous basis. Then, within each group, you can select a small group of children who need specific guidance. However, for many activities, the children will belong to the larger group and not feel segregated.

2. Assess all children at various points throughout the year using a range of diagnostic instruments. This includes observing each child's ability to use strategies to determine meaning with print.
3. For children learning to read or who are having difficulty reading, we can group and regroup children for short periods where, with peers who share similar reading skills, they focus on an applicable topic or skill.
4. Assess texts to determine if they meet the needs of the children who will read them. As a consequence, reading lists should vary from group to group, and there should be a variety of texts available to each group.
5. Allow for children's preferences in forming groups, which can include working with friends, exploring in depth a particular genre, or the work of an author.
6. Sometimes you can form groups based on reading speed. This will not necessarily result in a group whose reading abilities are similar.
7. At other times, you can form groups based on how children respond to text. When you group children who respond in various ways to a text, it helps those children who appear bound to one response mode.
8. All members of the class should view groups as flexible. Groups change on a regular basis and for a variety of reasons.

30: Guided Reading Instruction

Guided reading involves grouping children who have similar reading abilities or who need to acquire similar strategies for reading success. Unlike traditional reading groups, where membership is static, guided reading groups reform constantly throughout the year. The goal of these programs is to have all children read increasingly sophisticated texts – fiction and non-fiction alike – and develop strategies they can use independently. A supportive atmosphere is crucial to guided reading, as is ongoing observation and assessment. Children understand that throughout the day, groups will be dynamic and that they will work in a variety of configurations. Guided reading activities should develop into literature circles and book talk sessions in the years following primary.

Forming Groups

The process of building groups that work is one that evolves. A sound knowledge of each child in the class is needed. We must observe and assess children's ability on an ongoing basis, and note the processes and strategies they use to read. We can gather together children in groups that are flexible, whose members share a similar level of reading achievement and/or use of strategies, and where the children feel comfortable sharing their thoughts and reactions. It is recommended that a maximum of four groups be established in the class. If there are more groups than this, the process of text selection and working with the groups will become too cumbersome and impossible to manage.

Throughout the day, children will be working within other heterogeneous groups. Through the year, groups will change continuously. Ongoing observation and assessment of each child helps to determine his or her group placement. Running records, which can be done comfortably with one or two children per group each day, contribute to this ongoing assessment.

Choosing Appropriate Texts

Just as important as grouping the children correctly is the process of selecting appropriate texts. These texts, which should reflect the members' ages and interests, must be accessible: children should be able to read each text with the strategies they have on hand. At the same time, texts should contain sufficient new information that children will further their learning by reading them. Ideally, each text will be suited to practising a particular strategy.

At all levels, the reading component of the session should vary from five to ten minutes. Text length, then, should reflect this time span. Emergent and early readers can read texts with a maximum of 16 pages while more fluent readers can read short stories, selections from longer texts, non-fiction selections, and poems. Each child must have his or her own copy of the text.

A text that is too difficult will result in children calling out words with little or no comprehension. Such a situation does nothing to improve their reading ability or problem-solving strategies, and causes children unnecessary and avoidable anxiety. Reading a text that is too simple, while certainly less detrimental, does not ask children to apply their learning – it may be pleasurable but they may not grow from the experience.

Remember that each child in a group must have his or her own copy of the text. Two solutions are language arts anthologies, many of which contain fine pieces of literature, or language arts series that package multiple copies of popular children's reading. This is not to suggest that a class library consist of only language arts anthologies; rather, they can represent one component of a rich language program that draws on material from a variety of sources. Other benefits of using anthologies include the following:
• they offer support to developing readers,
• they reassure parents who are more comfortable with a structured approach to teaching,
• many series offer support activities, as well as suggestions for related literature,
• many series contain classic stories that are no longer available or are difficult to find in commercial forms,

• language arts series are lock-step only if used that way – selecting texts according to children's needs and interests ensures a sound, more natural approach to teaching reading.

Introducing Children to Guided Reading Sessions

Prior to having children take part in a guided reading session, you may want to teach them some routines that will be a part of their guided reading experience; for example, quietly moving from one classroom activity to another. You will need to set up well-organized routines to assist the children in knowing how to handle themselves while you're working with a small group of children in a guided reading session. Establishing group skills, and skills associated with independent learning (e.g., using the class library) will contribute to their guided reading experience.

If you are working with emergent readers, you may want to begin initial guided reading sessions by holding a single copy of the book while introducing it to the children. The introduction, which should take no longer than five minutes, should vary with each book and the group's needs and interests. Informal in tone, the introduction can consist of showing and discussing pictures and story patterns, the children making predictions about the text, providing glimpses of the plot, discussing potentially challenging words and concepts (but not "pre-teaching" vocabulary), outlining strategies children can use as an aid to reading the text, and discussing the intent of the reading. Chart these notes so that you and the children can refer to them after reading.

The introduction serves several purposes: it alerts children to text features; it provides them with a sense of useful strategies they can use to read the text; and it (hopefully) entices them to read the book. The overarching goal, then, is to provide children with enough information about the text so that they will be ensured of a successful reading experience.

During the Reading
Silent reading may be difficult for some emergent readers. Instead, they can read softly to themselves – the low pitch should not interfere or disrupt other readers. As they become able, they can read silently.

Observe children as they read. If you notice a child experiencing difficulty with vocabulary or content, and this difficulty prevents him or her from understanding the story, you can intercept quickly, keeping in mind the need for the child to continue reading. As well, you can ask a child to read aloud quietly so you can note strategies she or he uses, as well as other issues related to reading. Make a brief note on each child in the group.

The main focus of guided reading is making meaning with text. Children construct meaning before they read, as they read, and after they have read. Given that children in a guided reading group share similar reading levels and use of strategies, most if not all members should be able to read and understand the majority of the text being used. Their use of strategies helps them understand new information, whether it is vocabulary, contextual details, or structure.

Discussing the Reading

A crucial component of any guided reading session is the time devoted to discussion of the text – identifying aspects the children related to, discussing interesting vocabulary they met in the reading, assessing the accuracy of their predictions, identifying ways in which the text relates to their life, and sharing reactions and insights. Points listed on the chart created co-operatively prior to the reading can be discussed and new notes suggested by the children can also be added. Some readers will finish before their peers. These children can review some of the points on the chart as well as questions you have listed.

Discussions about the text can range from five minutes (emergent readers) to ten minutes (more able readers). We can direct children's attention to points in the text that support their knowledge (e.g., sound-letter relationships), or we can ask them to apply strategies. Together, we can revisit parts of the text or do a second reading of a text to help children increase fluency. Children can discuss their use of strategies when reading, including how they understand the text and strategies they need to develop further.

Finally, we need to ensure that children have access to the text after the reading session. They may choose to read the book again in class, or they may wish to take it home to read with a family member.

Following the Discussion

After the discussion, there are several options: 1) direct the group to other activities; 2) do a running record with one or more children from the group; and/or 3) provide extension activities that further their knowledge of topics related to the text. This last point is particularly relevant when working with texts that explore a concept that children want to learn about. Examples of extension activities include role play, art, researching the topic at the library, drawing story maps, and contrasting aspects of the story with a similar story. Guided reading encounters support and are connected to the language and literacy program in a classroom.

Evaluating a Guided Reading Program

Assessing a guided reading program is like assessing the growth of children: it is ongoing. In a guided reading program, we can assess our program by the success of the children's development and whether they are becoming successful, independent readers. We can ask ourselves these questions: Are the children flourishing in their reading program? Are they becoming readers who delight in the act of reading? Do they happily anticipate reading sessions? Do they choose to read independently?

Criteria for Classroom Books for Guided Reading Groups

Working with colleagues in your division, you can begin to develop a school-wide core collection of books. Shared experiences of books can be of great benefit to all teachers, especially those teachers new to the profession or new to the grade level.

To begin, meet as a large group and bring along books that you have used with children in a variety of situations and have proved beneficial – the children learn from reading the books and they enjoy them. Discuss how you used the books and indicate the audience for these books. Together, sort through all books determining categories for each – literature circles, read alouds, guided reading, and independent reading. Once books have been categorized, you can begin to organize by level of difficulty (e.g., topic, strategies needed to read books, degree of support

Key Elements of a Guided Reading Session with Young Readers

1. Group children who share a similar reading level for this particular activity.
2. Choose an appropriate text for the group that will lead to reading success.
3. Ask the children to sit in a circle.
4. Introduce the text by looking at its pictures (especially with emergent readers) and discuss a few potentially difficult words, the concepts, and the purpose of the reading.
5. Ask children to read the text silently, if possible, and independently.
6. Observe them as they read the text. Make notes of your observations.
7. At the end of the reading, discuss the book with the children – its plot, vocabulary, and concepts and especially the reading strategies they used. If suitable, children can take part in an extension activity, such as talking as if they were characters, or drawing the setting of the story.
8. Focus on rereading parts of the text as necessary for the discussion.
9. Draw attention to word patterns and sentence patterns to help in identifying unfamiliar words.
10. Sometimes you can cut sentences, phrases, and words from the story and have the children reconstruct the text.
11. Complete a running record with one child per group
12. Assess the children's development. Note those who need to move to another group.

Five Benefits of Guided Reading

1. Children can develop strategies that will help them grow as readers, now and in the years to come.
2. Children will have the opportunity to develop both individual skills (reading) and co-operative skills (as members of a group).
3. Children can read aloud to or with their peers in response to having read the text, not for assessment purposes but for the pleasure of reading aloud a piece of literature that appeals to them.
4. Children are immersed in reading in a comfortable environment where their learning, their opinions, and their reactions are valued.
5. Guided reading sessions present opportunities for us, as teachers, to capitalize on teachable moments and observe the children as they are reading and responding in a relaxed, familiar environment.

offered by visual cues, language, degree of prediction, repetition). Then, record the books in a log, including title, author, suggested level, and a brief summary of the book.

Try the books out in the classroom, adjusting designations on occasion. Note the success of the book with the children and the learning experiences it offered. You'll soon discover that some books that are a hit with one group may not be as well-received in another.

Every few months, reconvene to share experiences and reorganize the books. The vast array of quality children's literature – fiction and non-fiction – now available means that you have a ready supply of new books to add to the school collection.

1. Guided reading books must appeal to the children. They must invite the children into the world of story, whether through humor, connections to the children's lives, or through captivating plot lines.
2. Young readers need texts that reflect the language they hear. The texts should be in a readable font and should not overpower the reader. Books should be accompanied by supportive visual cues so that the children are assured of reading success, an important factor at this level. In addition, we can create books that capitalize on children's interests, vocabulary, and reading strengths.
3. Many of our classrooms are microcosms of our multicultural societies. We need to include literature that reflects cultures from around the world and is free of racial and gender stereotyping.
4. Books for guided reading need to span the varied interests of children in the class – from humor and sports through biographies and drama.
5. While each member of a group will share a similar reading ability, there will be some variation among members. Books chosen for guided reading should appeal to a range of abilities.
6. Books in a collection can share common elements. This increases children's comfort level and helps them to begin to look for links in reading.

7. Just as we look for quality in children's writing, we need to look for books that are representative of fine design. We need to present children with a variety of texts so that they are acquainted with a range of design factors.

To help children read, we need to create environments in which they

e	enjoy reading
n	need to read for meaning
c	connect texts they have read to their world and what they know
o	own their reading
u	use strategies and skills to develop new knowledge and skills
r	respond to their reading in supportive, literate environments
a	apply their reading skills with confidence
g	gain independence in reading
e	extend their learning
m	meet with success, even when reading texts that are challenging
e	evaluate their successes and identify areas for growth
n	negotiate new texts with sufficient support
t	talk about what they read in a supportive, encouraging environment

Levelling a Set of Core Books for Guided Reading

Classroom libraries can be organized in a variety of ways (see above) and books in these libraries need not be graded. Books used for guided reading, however, must be grouped according to level of difficulty, for this part of the program with young children. The most important consideration in assigning a level to a book rests on whether children at the level can read at a rate of 90-95 percent accuracy. For each level, there should be several books. If we were to organize groups in a class that were exact in terms of their reflection of children's reading abilities, we would likely end up with countless groups. Instead, we need to group children whose abilities, knowledge, and experience are similar. For this reason, our groups will contain a range of readers and the books we choose for them must reflect this reality. At the early reading level, these differences in text will be small. At the emergent level, differ-

ences will be greater, and they will be greater still at the developing level.

Guided reading collections can take time to build. To begin, you will likely need the help of colleagues, including the school librarian, to find copies of the same book (book sales can also be a good source). Selections of school anthologies represent another source of reading material.

Multiple Copies of Texts
1. In the primary grades, an important teaching objective is to create a community of readers. Assisting the children with selecting effective reading materials that can be shared is crucial as they develop as readers and thinkers.
2. In most patterned texts, the stories lend themselves to patterning. The text then becomes a skeleton or taking-off point for additional learning by the children.
3. Reading the same text helps to set the stage for young readers to achieve the skills they will require in becoming independent readers.

31: Establishing Literature Circles

One has only to look at the proliferation of adult book circles to appreciate the need to discuss what we read. When we, and the children, talk to others about our reading experiences, we can reveal our perceptions of the book, clarify concepts we found confusing, develop new perceptions based on those of our fellow readers, and take part in a shared, enjoyable experience that extends our personal and intellectual lives.

Literature circles allow children to engage in this type of book talk. As they discuss aspects of their reading – their predictions, perceptions, and responses – they understand what they have read at a much deeper level, and can relate their reading to their personal lives and to the prior knowledge they already have.

There are many benefits to using literature circles: children take charge of their learning; they improve listening and comprehension skills; and children who are reading below level gain in self-esteem through participating equally with their peers. Generally, literature circles give children the opportunity to appreciate that everyone has a point of view and each member has the opportunity to speak and be heard.

A literature circle typically comprises three to five children who are reading the same book and who gather together in small heterogeneous groups to discuss, read, and share responses. The purpose of the circle is to promote reading and encourage response to literature through discussions, and to provide opportunities for children to work in small groups that are usually child-centred. Children read the text silently – material is read aloud only to clarify a particularly confusing point, to support a point made in the discussion group, or to celebrate the author's style.

Guidelines for Literature Circles

1. Choose multiple copies of quality children's literature from a variety of genres.
2. Children listen as you provide introductions to each of the books.
3. Children then choose the book they want to read.
4. They find fellow class members who have chosen the same book. An ideal group size is five; it should never be larger than eight.
5. Children form a literature circle.
6. You can work with the children to determine how much text they will read each day and when and where they will meet.
7. Children read the text, and record their thoughts in a journal. Their responses to the text can take many forms, including notes, questions, and drawings.
8. They meet with fellow group members to discuss their experience with the reading. They can talk about any number of topics related to their reading, including challenging concepts, ways in which the book relates to what they know, puzzling questions, the use of literary devices, and so on.
9. Children may play a variety of roles in the group (e.g., the questioner, the summarizer) to help the discussion grow.
10. As the teacher, you can occasionally work as a facilitator for the group, helping members to stay on task, extending discussions, offering mini-lessons where needed, sometimes acting as a participant.
11. The success of the literature circles is evaluated both by the children and the teacher.

Getting Started

Literature circles may take time to establish. Introducing, explaining, and demonstrating the concept of a literature circle, as well as modelling good questioning and discussion behavior, provide the appropriate atmosphere for success. A literature circle discussion chart can prompt and spark discussion, and may include some of the following:

- talk about the book's title and author,
- discuss what has been read,
- identify favorite parts of a book, and reasons for these choices,
- read aloud bits from the journals,
- list topics for the next discussion.

Picture books can be used to introduce the concept of a literature circle. Then, children can explore the concept by using a novel the whole class is reading. We need to choose the book carefully for the first sessions. As time progresses, we can encourage children to choose from among three or four books, giving them some control over their learning.

When organizing literature circles for the first time, it can be wise to assign children to a group. However, once children become familiar with literature circles, they can form their own groups as they choose a novel from the preselected selections. Your role is now that of observer and evaluator, problem solver and facilitator. You can monitor the groups, and may join a group to add to the discussion.

Before beginning to read, the children can engage in an introductory activity, such as answering a survey or a list of questions, taking part in a cloze activity, or completing a "What I know about... ." Children should understand that oral reading occurs only when a concept needs to be clarified or when beginning readers or other children need assistance. If possible, you can make a tape of the book and place it in the listening centre for those who may need assistance with the text.

To help children become accustomed to participating fully in literature groups, they can take on roles, vary the duties, and eliminate them when they are no longer needed. Children can do their silent reading in class, and discussions can follow after they have completed a small chunk of the text. Group members can decide on what to read next and how much they will cover. (Some readers-at-risk may need to listen to a taped version as they read to prepare for the discussion.)

Roles for Children

Instigator	raises issues for the group to discuss based on the day's reading
Linguist	draws group's attention to interesting words in the story (notes the page number) and discusses their meaning with the group
Literary Artist	chooses an event or mood conveyed in the reading and illustrates it for the group (can add to a collection of day's pictures)
Literary Critic	finds examples of effective literary techniques in passage, effective passages and, conversely, passages that are problematic
Questioner	presents puzzling issues raised in the day's reading for the group to consider, relating to personal response, as well as questions relating to content
Reteller	summarizes the day's reading for the group
Text Enricher	supports the text by bringing in other related stories or non-fiction articles, books by the same author, or books set in the same place or during the same time period

The Role of Journals

Journals are an integral part of literature circles. They are the first place children respond to the material they have read and can be indispensable in literature circles, as the children use them to demonstrate their ideas, raise issues, clarify points, or as support for an arguments. In their journals, children can record their reactions to books they are reading, their reading goals, problems or puzzles posed by the book, reactions to discussions, and questions they would like to talk about with their peers.

Time devoted to journals should be built into the schedule so that children can come to the group with their reading and journal entries completed. Journals can be used as both follow-up to the discussion and as preparation and guiding statements during the next discussion.

Schedules

There are several ways a reading program can be structured to accommodate literature circles. For example, if there are four reading groups in your class, each group can participate in a literature circle several times a week. Other options include having groups hold a literature circle on two days of the week, or the group can participate in a literature circle on an as-needed basis.

Ideally, literature groups can meet three times per week for a period of fifteen to thirty minutes, lasting from one day to six weeks, depending on the length of a book. With chapter books, children usually meet following each silent reading session.

Modifying Assignments

Like adults, children need to work within reasonable deadlines. They need to have long-term goals established at the outset of the reading program, and short-term goals set daily and weekly that will help them meet long-term goals. Contracts are a useful device to help children comprehend the work they must do in order to achieve their goals.

Ensuring Good Discussions

When any group convenes, invariably one or two people will dominate the discussion. To circumvent this situation in a literature circle, work with each group on how to hold profitable discussions. Outline how the literature circle works and stress the importance of positive group behavior. Assign roles according to the chart above.

Initially, each child can be given a token, which they trade in for an opportunity to speak. This structure is particularly effective for younger children, or for children who are inexperienced in such work situations. Older children, more accustomed to working as part of a group, may be able to conduct the group on their own, with you working as an equal member of the group.

Model for the children statements that can help to extend a discussion. The statements should focus on the positive and should not resemble questions. Examples include:
- I agree with _____. I think that....
- I agree with _____ because...
- I disagree with _____ because...
- What does the author mean...
- I found this part confusing because...

Audiotaping or videotaping a session can help you to observe the dynamics of the group and the literacy behavior of its members. As well, the group can use the tape after completing discussions on the book and reflect on their contributions and the process. An assessment meeting can be held to consider modifying how the members are working, and each member can self-reflect using his or her journal. Children talk, read, write, and think for real purposes. Such self-regulating management takes time to establish. Periodic whole-class discussions can generate guidelines to help children function and grow from the process.

Create a menu of choices, which children can refer to during the course of the talk, marking passages children can share, modelling responses, using past examples done by children, and encouraging children to respond to the selection through art or graphics.

Our Role in Literature Circles

Our role as teachers is to extend the learning that children experience in literature circles. Freed of the limitations of responding to set questions, these groups offer children the chance to pursue lines of inquiry that satisfy their needs as readers and learners. We can help them by ensuring that they delve into the text, that their efforts are supported through mini-lessons and conferences, and that they focus on aspects of the text that will extend their scope and experience. We can

- choose quality literature that children will both enjoy and learn from,
- monitor the children, intervening in the form of mini-lessons and conferences when needed,
- help children take responsibility for their success and that of the group by drafting conduct and management policies with the children,
- encourage children to move beyond simple retelling so that they can apply higher-order thinking skills – they can analyze, critique, compare, assess, and evaluate,
- help children to become independent thinkers and learners who take ownership and pride in their learning.

As they begin working in their literature circles, you will need to help children form groups and choose the books to be read. In addition, you will need to be a member of each group at some time,

helping children to stay on task and explore the book in a meaningful way. It is important, when participating in discussions, to refrain from asking directed questions. Questions, particularly those that require short answers, can direct the route of a conversation, and make the person who asks them the centre of attention. Statements, on the other hand, extend the conversation and retain the group's equilibrium. Consider the implication of the question "What did you notice about...." with the statement "The author made me think about...." In this way, you can have the children consider a point without adding the stress of answering the question correctly. By participating in a discussion in such a way, children absorb techniques that extend discussions and allow group members to contribute freely. Children will soon be able to conduct an effective literature circle without your participation.

This shift in interaction can be uncomfortable, at least initially, for both children and teachers. Discussions may be superficial – children will need time to practise conversation skills and time to explore facets of their reading that will lead to good discussions. Some children, particularly those that are shy, may have difficulty contributing to a discussion in which the standard rules of the classroom have changed. In these cases, you can encourage the children to tell you or another member their thoughts. In turn, you can share them with the group. As well, the children can make their contribution to the group by reading from their journal or having a friend read their words. Encourage an environment where these children will feel safe and where they can gradually begin to contribute to the group.

The transition will not be seamless and there may be a proliferation of silences that are abnormal in the typical classroom environment. Initially, you and the children will be more comfortable with a question-response environment in which you are viewed as the expert. Although it may be difficult, try to refrain from filling in when the conversation dwindles. Usually, it will begin again, but if it stretches on you can remind the children that this is their conversation and encourage them to take the lead.

You can use your decreased time in the circles to observe children at work. In fact, literature circles offer you an ideal time to assess when and how children may benefit from mini-lessons and conferences. Consider the following factors:

- the participants (their level of reading ability, group skills),
- how children enter the activity,
- how they choose the book,
- positions members take as they sit together,
- how decisions are made about how to proceed,
- use of the text,
- the frequency with which children examine the text,
- whether the talk resembles a conversation, a dialogue, a monologue,
- whether members take turns speaking,
- who speaks most frequently and who speaks the least,
- who initiates the discussion,
- how members explain their thinking,
- how members handle diverse opinions,
- how members discuss the author's style,
- whether members mention examples of interesting language use,
- if members demonstrate knowledge about how books work,
- the sharing of personal experiences and stories,
- if members make connections to the wider world,
- if members use what they have discovered in the literature circles in other activities.

Grouping for Literature Circles

Groups should be heterogeneous in nature with a maximum number of eight children per group (three to five is ideal). In large groups, some children will hesitate to voice their opinions. In groups of two or three, children do not benefit from a variety of input and opinions. When there are more than five children who want to read the same book, two groups may be formed. On occasion, children can benefit from whole-class discussions when each child has a copy of the same book – they can discuss a variety of factors, including elements of plot, language devices, setting, and characters, how the text relates to another they have read, stylistic details, and the work of the illustrator. They can listen to the wide-ranging opinions of their peers and witness first-hand how the experience of literature is a personal one.

Initially, arrange the children in groups. Each group should include a range of readers. The groups, like those in guided reading, change depending on the books selected by the children to ensure a mix of abilities. Eventually, children can choose the group they wish to join based on the introductions you provide for the books to be read.

Seating Arrangement

Literature circles can be formed around a table or on the floor. The circle shape ensures that no one person is seen as "head" of the group, including you – like other members of the group, you are there to contribute but not to run the circle. Equal seating for members has an impact on the group, as members can see that the process is not to be led by one person and judged according to his or her standards.

Text Considerations

Initially, you can choose the books children will read in literature circles. As they become more comfortable with the format, children can choose from the classroom library. Give each book a brief introduction that tantalizes the children into wanting to read it, but does not give the whole plot away. Children can listen to the introductions, then peruse the books before deciding on the one they would like to read. The books should appeal to children's sense of story.

As in guided reading, each child will need to have his or her personal copy of the book. Sources of books include the class and school libraries, public libraries, other teachers, and book clubs. You will also need a copy of the book in which you can write suggestions for enhancing their reading, interesting examples of vocabulary, or literary devices.

Children who have difficulty reading a text will benefit from listening to a tape recording of the book. It is not necessary that they be able to read every word – as long as they understand the gist of the story, they can participate in a literature circle. The experience can help to build their confidence when they see themselves as equal partners of more fluent readers.

Managing the Class

An important aspect of instituting literature circles is a set of easily understood management rules. You can work with the children to draft the rules. In this way, they will understand them and enforce them since they had a role in their evolvement. Through the process, you and the children should arrive at a set of rules such as these the following.

Management Techniques
1. Only one group should be in discussion. In this way, the group members can work in an atmosphere devoid of noisy interruptions. This also allows you to follow the discussion quite easily.
2. While one group discusses their reading, other children can work on activities related to the books they are reading and complete journal activities.
3. Those children who are working independently need to know that you will not be available to work with them.
4. If they need to talk to a classmate, they must whisper or use a low voice.
5. Children working independently need to work in one area of the classroom, preferably at a table or their desk.

When you and the children have decided on the rules, write them on a chart to be posted in the classroom. Discuss how rules can be modified during the school year as the need arises. Children will feel responsible for a classroom environment that they have put into place.

Rules for Individuals in Literature Circles
1. Make your contributions equal to that of other group members.
2. Each member has the same right to speak.
3. All opinions are equal.
4. Pay attention when someone speaks.
5. Look at the speaker when she or he talks.
6. Allow for differences of opinion.
7. Express disagreements in a positive way.
8. Do not speak when someone else is speaking.
9. Read the material you are assigned before joining the group.
10. Complete your journal work before joining the group.

Once the Program Is in Place

Once the program is established and the children are working comfortably in their circles, you can plan a meeting schedule. Depending on the age of your students and other schedule demands, you can structure this in any number of ways. Some teachers prefer to meet with each group on a daily basis, while others find that three meetings per week with each group are sufficient.

In terms of discussion time, most groups can hold a profitable discussion in a fifteen-minute time span. The length of a book, though, will determine the length of time the group devotes to it, which can vary from a day to six weeks.

Schedule time for children to read their book in class. Depending on the age of the readers, you can assign a number of pages or chapters. This time allowance can be more difficult if you are working with the whole class and/or are teaching at the intermediate and secondary school levels. A schedule that allows for shortened time periods includes having children read for two days in a row, then discuss for two days. The fifth day can be used as a general day for clearing up topics that were unresolved or pursuing independent research.

However you structure the program, you can consider making completed reading and journal entries a condition of participation. If a child has not read the required material going into a literature circle, she or he will have little to add and may distract others from their discussion. Completing journal assignments is equally important since children use their journals to back up their points in discussion, and as a reminder of questions they have regarding their reading.

Finally, as children work independently in their groups, you can provide them with some nonverbal support in the way of cues for discussion. You can list the following topics on a chart (many of these topics can serve as the focus for mini-lessons). Children can use it as a resource as they discuss a book:

Plot	Making Predictions
Characters	Drawing Conclusions
Mood	Identifying the Author's Voice
Setting	Comparing the Novel to Others
Vocabulary	(Genre, Author)
Illustrations	Connecting the Novel to the
Style	Real World
	Analyzing Strengths and
	Weaknesses
	Evaluating the Novel

What Children Gain from Literature Circles

There are a number of benefits of literature circles. Children considered to be at-risk see themselves as partners with more fluent readers. While their responses may at first be more superficial than their peers, they still contribute to the group and are viewed as equal members. In addition, many of these children are worried about being incorrect. In a literature circle, no answer is ignored. *All* children can allow themselves to interact with the text on a deeper level: they can question, disagree, agree, or change their opinion.

The social atmosphere of the class grows cohesive. Children work with all their peers through the year and are not relegated to one ability group. All children in the class are members of the group and all have voices that must be heard. This is an important concept when building a community of readers. In literature circles, children work together to construct something – meaning from text – co-operatively. The success of the venture is determined largely on each member's ability to work as part of a group. Children learn skills of co-operation as a group member, as well as the trust that develops when people share ideas and thoughts.

Children's understanding of books – how they are written, why they are written, how they make them feel, how they relate to the outside world – are expanded in literature circles where book talk on all levels is encouraged. The use of strong literature further enhances literature circles, and children begin to understand why reading is, for some, a lifelong affair filled with pleasure.

The classroom becomes a place of shared decision making. The children have contributed to the drafting of conduct and management policies and therefore have an interest in seeing that they are maintained. This includes taking responsibility for how the class and groups are run and for their own contribution to the group's well being.

Evaluation

Evaluation of literature circles involves consideration of several elements: the level of discussion that occurs in the literacy circles, the children's social behavior, and their growth as readers and writers.

To assess the quality of discussion, you can tape several circles over the course of the week. Together with the group members and on your own, review the tapes. Listen for overriding comments, lack of listening skills, superficial talk, and so on. Play back relevant sections and discuss with children positive and negative elements of the discussion. Together, plan steps the group can take to improve the discussion. In addition, children need to look at their own role in the literature circle. Did they make valuable contributions to the discussion? What strengths do they bring to a literature circle? What areas do they need to develop?

Assessing interests and attitudes will tell us much about how we are meeting our goals of helping children become lifelong readers. This includes assessing the amount of reading the child does in addition to that of literature circles, in and out of school. Can the child easily identify aspects in reading that were once challenging? Does the child exhibit development in his or her reading and writing practices?

32: Reading with the Whole Community

As teachers, we can contribute to the sense of community by providing plenty of opportunities to read aloud to them, often, materials they normally would not experience. Chapter books and novels, for example, read a section at a time, can become a high point of the day, and a time when children can anticipate gathering together to hear the next installment. When we choose books that support a theme, we can extend children's learning; when we read newspaper and magazine articles, we can model how to find content information and how to stay abreast of current events.

There are many ways in which the reading can take place – we, as teachers, can lead the discussion and model the use of strategies (how to question a text, and how to raise discussion issues); children can read silently; the group can read the book aloud; children can read the text with a partner; or agreed-upon pages can be read together and others silently. While the notion of whole-class guided reading can be problematic, such sessions can offer unique chances to observe children in a large-group setting – their level of participation, their ability to follow a discussion, their ability to raise relevant issues, and their use of strategies for understanding. As well, you can demonstrate how books work.

Crucial to the process of whole-class guided reading is an open, accepting attitude where children feel free to respond without fear of errors. This is particularly true in large-group discussions where some children are intimidated by the size of the group. While the reading may be done as a large group, children can work in small groups, with a partner, or independently to do follow-up work, including discussing the material read and responding in their journals. These smaller groups allow shy children the chance to contribute to the large group's discussion.

Talking and Writing as a Class

To set the stage for reading, children can share personal experiences of the topic explored in the text. They can make predictions based on the introduction and on pragmatic cues. Children can raise questions they have about the topic or story, and record them, as well as their predictions, in their journal.

As the reading progresses, children look for confirmation of their predictions and answers to their questions. Discussions can occur during key intervals during the story and at the end of the day's reading. To help children explore the text at a deeper level, we can guide their learning by asking questions that have them think critically and creatively. Children can write their responses to the story in their journals, including how predictions were confirmed, which questions were answered, how other questions need to be modified given events in the text, interesting vocabulary they discovered, their personal response to story, and how it, or parts of it, relate to their life. In most instances, children will share their journals with us. Before they can do this confidently, we can work with them to develop an atmosphere of trust. They need to understand that their opinion is personal and therefore as significant as that of

their peers or teacher. As well, journals represent private thoughts, and so children need to know that we are going to respect their privacy.

Response Activities

Follow-up activities should reinforce and extend children's understanding of the text: writing back cover copy for a proposed sequel; writing an additional chapter using the voice of the author; preparing a timeline for a character's life; role-playing Siskel and Ebert (review the book as a movie); writing and role-playing a dialogue between two characters; presenting a tableaux that represents the turning point or main event in the story; and planning music and special effects that could accompany a taped version of the text. From working with the whole class at times, the energy and ideas can motivate individuals to continue independently.

33: Individualized Reading

In individualized reading, children are encouraged to read at their own pace using materials they have chosen to read. Our role reflects this goal – rather than modelling behaviors and guiding children in the reading process, we become observers of and audiences for children's reading. In some programs, individualized reading represents the core of the program; in others, it will be one of many components. Regardless of its place in the program, individualized reading sessions should include the following characteristics:
- Children choose the material they want to read. As teachers, we can give advice and help if asked, but it is up to the children to decide what they will read from a selected library of books.
- Children need to be able to select from quality literature, fiction and non-fiction alike. We do not select their texts, but we can help to ensure that they read the finest of literature available by including such books in our class and school library. As the children's tastes change, so, too should the library. We also need to ensure that the books reflect curriculum concerns.
- Children read at their own pace.

- Children have plenty of opportunity to read in class. Since reading levels are dependent in large part on time and opportunity to read, we must provide time in class, particularly for children who are not reading at home.
- Help should be available when children need it. Our assistance can take a variety of forms, from conferences to a small-group demonstration.
- Children need to have brief conferences with the teacher during the week.
- Children need to be encouraged to develop an awareness of the variety of resources.
- Accurate, up-to-date records of the books children have read, as well as information about their progress in reading, must be kept through the year. During conferences, we can note strategies each child uses, areas of strengths, and areas that need to be developed. Children can record in their journals books they have read, their reactions to the books, observations they have made during reading, words they have learned, and how they've responded to their reading.

Selecting Books for the Classroom

Our goal as teachers is to encourage all children to read. At each stage in their development, we must provide them with reading materials that match their abilities and continue to develop their appetite for literature.

This goal is especially challenging at the early primary level, when one or two additional lines of text can intimidate a young reader. Issues of a readable font, spacing, and supportive illustrations need to be considered. We should exercise particular caution when matching these children to texts. Conferences and observing their reading interests can prove invaluable in this task.

Finding suitable reading materials for older children can also be challenging. For example, children in middle elementary grades often want to read novels, but may be hampered by extensive text. In this instance, we can look for novels that have fewer words per page, some illustrations, and a greater number of chapters. Children who are emerging readers should have the opportunity to read literature that contains frequently used words. That said, the vocabulary should not be artificially controlled and the children should be encouraged to reread these texts for fluency.

The Classroom Library

While children will read books from the public and school libraries, we need to have on hand a core of books that reflect the abilities and interests of all children in the class. How do we choose these books when there are literally thousands of contenders?

We need to represent a wide genre of books, including novels, short stories, poetry, non-fiction books, cultural stories, myths, folktales, and picture books. Some should be classics, but most should be contemporary stories. In addition to books, we need to have on hand suitable magazines, selected newspapers, and taped books. All of the resources we choose should be familiar to us and should support children in their reading development.

When Children Choose

In a classroom library, there will be a wide selection of books, carefully chosen to support the needs and wishes of the children. Children make choices from this collection for individualized reading time, and for guided reading occasions. When a child chooses a book, she or he takes responsibility for learning. Children usually select a book because they are interested in the topic. Therefore, whether the book reflects their reading ability may be secondary, since interest can motivate a child to read a book that may be difficult. The fact that we let children choose shows that we have trust in their abilities. We can then support their reading through discussions, conferences, and mini-lessons and demonstrations, should the children need to tap into strategies to enrich the reading experience.

We need to consider that certain types of books can offer additional support to readers, including books where a child is familiar with the characters from reading previous books in the series. They know the author's style of writing, and can make predictions based on past experiences with his or her work. Non-fiction books can explore a topic with which children are very familiar and want to read. As well, most non-fiction books contain photographs, diagrams, illustrations, and subheadings that support the text.

Through the year, we can encourage the children to experience a range of genres by providing introductions that motivate them to read books. In addition, we can help them to refine their selection process by asking them to discuss books with peers, read reviews, and sample a text they are considering reading. Children can also share their selection strategies in a large-group discussion. Chances are that common themes will emerge, including recommendations of friends, works by favorite authors, books on favorite topics, the connections they share with a book, and the attraction of the covers and book design. All are reasons for selecting a book, and all can lead to reading a range of texts.

Setting Up a Program

Focused, independent reading programs require planning and commitment on our part, and large amounts of time when children can read silently and reflect on what they have learned. During individualized reading, children need to read a range of meaningful texts that will extend their reading abilities. To ensure their success, children should be able to read approximately 90 percent of words in a text independently. That said, if a child truly wants to read a difficult book, it is best to warn him or her that it may be difficult and let the child attempt the book – sometimes the will to read a book and a high level of interest in the topic help the child to master a text that is above his or her level

A reading corner can provide a focus for reading. Independent selection depends on an environment that allows for opportunities of choice to be present in varied and enriched contexts. The opportunity to read is also extended through tapes children can listen to, both at home and school.

A child's concentration can be extended over time, as can the level and range of reading material. When a child's sustained silent reading demonstrates developed interest in reading, we have been successful in guiding the reader toward independence. To achieve this, it is important to match the child and the book in reading instruction. Reading at a level of proficiency encourages the development of positive attitudes and confidence. Many graded-reader manuals provide information on how to determine a child's reading level. It is important to teach skills at a level that permits independence and success.

Initially, short daily sustained silent reading periods are best. A quiet time without interruption can be extended from five minutes at the kindergarten-grade 1 level to thirty minutes at the grade 6 level. If the children are aware of their responsibilities during these periods, they are more likely to persevere with their reading. When they run into difficulty, we can discuss with them strategies such as skipping the word or thinking about what would make sense. We can model procedures of skill development, especially in a one-on-one context when a problem arises.

In kindergarten or grade 1, you can modify your program by distributing picture books and books children have heard read aloud. Initially, children cannot be expected to read independently – they need encouragement and practice in class routines that will require your help to work as part of a group and on an individual basis. Some will prefer to read as part of a small group or with a friend. Whatever the situation, children need to appreciate the need for creating a quiet time for reading. When they have internalized criteria for independent work and a reading environment has been established, a successful sustained silent reading program has been put in place.

In later grades, the independent reader becomes the owner of his or her reading experience, and will be stimulated and rewarded by selecting books for personal reading. We need to explain, demonstrate, and have children practise the skill of selecting books that are of an appropriate reading level and genre. Older children can be taught the "five-finger" technique that involves reading a page and curling one finger into the palm each time a difficult word is encountered. If, at the end of the passage, she or he has curled five or fewer fingers the book is approximately the correct reading level.

Young children can also be made aware of the deceptive level of some books. Text, and not illustrations, is the major criterion in determining reading difficulty.

The importance of children selecting appropriate books needs to be emphasized. The independent reader may read during the reading period, in his or her spare time in the classroom, go to the library voluntarily, talk about books with other children, complete reading assignments promptly, and order books from paperback book clubs.

Independent readers can keep track of their reading, encouraging comparison of authors and texts and the development of focused reading habits. Reading journals and reading logs offer formal techniques for tracking children's reading experiences.

Teaching situations may occur whenever the opportunity or occasion arises, but may be especially focused in individualized reading conferences. The conference represents an opportunity for us to assess the child's learning process and to participate in a shared activity in which opinions and perceptions serve as the topics from which assessment is gathered.

Uninterrupted sustained silent reading (USSR), periods where children can read uninterrupted, are effective components of a reading program. Knowing that they will not be stopped during their reading helps children to concentrate, and the practice is strengthened when we schedule a set time for USSR each day. Some children, particularly in the younger grades, may prefer to work with a partner or a small group. In these instances, as in similar instances throughout the independent reading program, children need to understand the need for a quiet atmosphere.

34: The Preadolescent Reader

The years between eight and thirteen are often referred to as the quantity years. Children at this age will read a range of materials, including novels, biographies, books in a series and sports stories. It is during this time that many children identify and refine their literary tastes, and many will have favorite genres and authors. These children need to have a wide range of books from which to choose, and we need to draw their attention to other books they may not have considered to help them broaden their knowledge and reading experience. When designing a program for older readers, we need to consider the following factors:

1. We need to know our children's tastes in books – their favorite authors and genres – as well as their reading abilities so that we may build a classroom library that reflects their interests and needs.
2. We need to establish an atmosphere that is conducive to reading. There should be quiet corners and areas in the class where children can settle in comfortably to read independently.
3. The books we supply for these children must include a number of new books, as well as old stand-bys that children like to return to on occasion. The class library should contain, in addition to fiction, a variety of non-fiction books. While materials should challenge the children, they should contain sufficient familiar vocabulary and concepts so that children can read them independently.
4. We need to build in time during the day to conference with children so that we can discuss their reading, new challenges they would like to attempt, and gains they have made in their development.
5. Some children will have reached a level where they are able to read adult fiction. We can help these children by providing them with novels that reflect their age and maturity at the same time as they present the children with sophisticated plot lines. Often children miss reading the wonderful young adult novels written by excellent authors for their age group. Teachers can bring these books to the attention of youngsters who are ready to read them.
6. Children at this age are beginning to take part in extracurricular activities, so time for reading can become an issue. For children who are at risk, this can be a troublesome reality. We need to build in time to the day's schedule to ensure that children continue to read in depth.
7. A school that provides parents with book lists and connects parents with all aspects of the child's reading program will find support at home that encourages and promotes reading growth. The Internet provides several resources for children's literature updates.

The Importance of Novels

Novels for children and young adolescents allow intensive and extensive experiences in reading, where children step outside their lives to identify and reflect on human behaviors, emotions, values, and conflicts. The reader becomes a participant drawn into the story, experiencing the lives of its characters. As children develop their reading abilities, they come to appreciate a story, not only by identifying with the characters but by seeing the story through the eyes of the author. By reading and responding to novels, children are able to see how authors use their talents and techniques to create stories. Children also come to understand and appreciate the style, language, plot, and characters that are found in novels.

For some children, novels help to answer questions related to aspects of their own lives. When we group novels around a theme, children experience a part of their existence through the portrayal of others who are experiencing similar circumstances. Novels, then, can be a confirmation of life for young readers. For other children, novels represent an entry into a fantasy world far removed from their time and experience. Novels have the power to influence the literary and literacy lives of their readers. As teachers, we can surround children with quality literature that invites them to read. The goal of encouraging all children to become lifelong readers is easier when they realize the satisfaction and power reading can offer.

In the classroom, novels can be read silently and independently or as part of a group. In some instances, children will be content to read the novel and not take part in response activities – their response may consist of quiet reflection of what they have read. In other instances, novels will lead to a range of response activities as children dig deeper into their experience to further their understanding. They can respond through drama, art, discussion, and research. These activities may lead them to analyze, compare, problem solve, and share all goals of a literacy classroom.

When children choose novels, they:
- listen to the recommendation of friends,
- look for works by favorite authors,
- look for works in a favorite genre,
- look for novels that reflect personal issues,
- look for novels that provide escape from their lives,
- look for novels that can help them learn about their own lives,
- consider the length of the novel,
- consider the attractiveness of the cover,
- consider whether their peers would read it.

35: Supporting the Reader in Difficulty

Readers in difficulty need:
- programs that stress strategies for growth,
- extensive support as they extend their abilities,
- additional one-on-one conferring and demonstrations,
- texts that are predictable and that contain easily discernible patterns (especially for younger readers),
- opportunities to build letter and word patterns,
- opportunities to incorporate new sight words into their speech and writing,
- time to respond to the reading selection,
- opportunities to reread texts, both for pleasure and for the development of fluency,
- encouragement to develop literary habits – browsing, reviewing, selecting – and encouragement to develop a personal taste in literature,
- opportunities to experience success in reading and bolster their confidence as readers,
- real reasons to read and write.

The factors that explain why these children are at risk are as varied as the children themselves. Some may have medical difficulties, others home difficulties, still others attention deficit difficulties. Some children may learn at a slower rate than their peers, some may experience problems in particular areas, and some in all areas of learning. Some may progress at a "normal" pace, but become blocked at a particular point in their learning. Whatever the reason, we need to observe and assess the children to decide on the support they most need.

We need to spend time with these children individually or, for brief times, in small groups where they share the same level of literacy development. Together, we can read aloud to the children, read with the children, and listen to them read to us. We can help readers by giving them quiet reading time, by helping them to identify the purpose for reading, and by making obvious the link to activities to make the experience with print meaningful and real.

No matter what the quality or type of reading instruction, good readers will always manage to read. They take what makes sense from the program and disregard extraneous information. For their at-risk peers, however, several issues are important. At-risk readers benefit from intensive and sequential programs. However, they may be able to isolate sounds and read a word in isolation, but when they find that word in context, they cannot recognize it. Such readers need individual attention from us, as well as numerous chances to apply their reading in authentic contexts.

We need to present words in context and foster sight-word recognition, since fluent reading requires the automatic knowledge of many words. We can help children to connect words by selecting texts that integrate background knowledge and highlight their experiences, feelings, and interests. We can then begin to work with the words a child knows to develop strategies for recognizing and analyzing letters, clusters of letters, sound-symbol relationships, onsets and rimes, spelling peculiarities, and complicated or unfamiliar words.

Broadening print vocabulary is key to expanding the reader's world. Children can succeed by writing personal stories or journals, where we can then use their writing to focus their attention on the mechanics of writing, such as punctuation and spelling, and teach mini-lessons drawn from their problems.

At-risk readers need plenty of reinforcement. For example, we can run a finger along a line or let the child do the same so that she or he can track the reading progress. We can keep records of children's reading patterns, such as skipping words or letter reversals. However, we can also encourage creative thinking as the readers grow; helping them to develop as literate people who find reasons to read and meet success in their attempts.

Identifying the Reader in Difficulty*

- hesitates when asked to read because of past, negative experiences,
- lacks confidence as a reader and as a learner,
- has difficulty comprehending selected texts,
- has difficulty retelling a story,
- lacks knowledge of how books work and the characteristics that differentiate genres,
- may present erratic eye movements, has difficulty following a line, or rereads the same word,
- has reversals that continue into older grades,
- displays little initiative to read,
- has a small automatic sight-word vocabulary,
- makes illogical substitutions when reading aloud,
- has difficulty identifying a purpose for reading,
- has difficulty writing complex sentences,
- is inconsistent in his or her reading attempts,
- has mastered only a few reading strategies,
- uses one strategy to the exclusion of all others.

*Most children who have difficulty reading have a combination of some of these indicators

Tutoring Strategies

1. Introduce new books (of high interest) and at a level that the child can read successfully.
2. With the child, explore a book before reading so that the child is familiar with its style and content, has the opportunity to make personal connections to the text, and can make predictions based on the introduction, the cover, its title, and illustration.
3. At times, as in shared reading, we can read the story aloud as the child follows along with his or her copy, preparing the new reader with a general understanding of the text.
4. An at-risk reader may need to read or reread the text aloud in a one-on-one conference as we observe the strategies she or he uses. Given this knowledge, we can then extend his or her use of strategies through comments, questions, and demonstrations.
5. We can offer prompts for helping the child with structural words and questions like "When did that happen?" "What did they do?" The goal is to help the child discover particular words using all the available techniques.

6. We can demonstrate self-monitoring strategies that good readers use – thinking, predicting, sampling, confirming, self-correcting – by asking questions such as the following:
   - Does that word sound right?
   - Does it make sense in the story?
   - Skip the word and go on.
   - Does the word fit in the sentence?
   - Put in a word that makes sense.
   - Where have you seen that word before?
   - Do you know a word with the same sound in it?
   - Now what do you think it is?
   - What is the first letter? Does it help you? How will the word begin?
   - Check the word with the picture.

7. A child should be given enough time to figure out the word. We can point out word patterns that will help uncover a word from the knowledge the child already possesses, write a pattern for the word on the chart, present a rhyming word, or draw the child's attention to the word on an existing label or word wall. We can promote the context of the story to encourage word identification, calling attention to incidents and events in the story that incorporate the word, or note predictable and recurring patterns.

8. Focusing on phonics with a particular word can help the child to examine it carefully, notice how the letters and sounds work, make generalizations, and then restore it to the context of the text. We can follow up with related response activities that draw the child back to the text, extend understanding, increase word recognition, and foster knowledge of how words work.

9. We can help the child work with the text in a variety of ways:
   - promoting discussion about what the child has read before narrowing in on a skill follow-up,
   - encouraging sight-word recognition in context by writing high-frequency words from the text on cards so that the child can match them with the text, using context, patterns, and pictures,
   - creating a written innovation from the text where the child determines the pattern of the new text and the words it will contain. We can record his or her text on a chart for rereading. Later, the child can record the words in individual booklets that can be illustrated,
   - using an unfamiliar text to observe how the child applies strategies she or he uses for daily reading and writing behaviors.

10. We can take a sentence from a story a child has written or has just finished reading. By cutting the sentence up so that each word is on a piece of paper, the child can use the pieces and reorganize them to make a story, checking his or her work against the original when finished.

11. Predictable, well-written literature is particularly effective with a child who has experienced reading difficulty, both at the elementary and secondary levels. It is even more effective when children choose what they read. With more motivation to read, children have a real reason to learn the skills and strategies that will help them become fluent readers.

12. An at-risk reader can benefit from reading a number of predictable texts. When comfortable with the format, the child can model it in writing to make a predictable book. The child can illustrate the book and place it in the class library where others can read it.

13. A child can read the work of a favorite author, or work from a favorite genre. When familiar with the words, the child can use them as the basis for an original text that can be created with group members. Our role in this activity is to act as a recorder, if necessary, or as an audience. The child can prepare the sequel/story/poem/chapter in a number of formats, including as an illustrated copy, as an overhead, as a big book, as a dialogue between characters, as a monologue by the lead character, or as a mime.

14. Wordless picture books are an effective literacy tool at all grades. A child can tell the story orally, write the text, have a partner write the text, or create a picture book that builds on a published story.

15. When we read aloud to a child, we increase vocabulary and comprehension, introduce the child to a range of author styles and genres, and model fluent reading. All children need to have books read to them, including those at the secondary level, where the experience can help clarify the meanings of challenging words and ideas.

16. In repeated readings, a child practises reading one passage repeatedly until she or he can read it fluently (this will vary from child to child and depends on the degree of fluency, as well as accuracy). The benefits of repeated readings are numerous, particularly for at-risk readers, and carry over to other texts that they have not practised, helping to

increase fluency, word recognition, and comprehension. We need to give a child genuine reasons for reading and we need to make the activity enjoyable. We can achieve this in part by encouraging the child to choose a passage they want to read. Texts that lend themselves to this activity include picture books, poems, and short stories. When a child reads aloud to you, you can observe the strategies she or he employs. You can then discuss and model strategies that will further their reading development. As well, you can use the opportunity to take a running record in a one-to-one conference.

17. A child can read aloud to a partner who then gives feedback. Sessions should be short, between 10 to 15 minutes a day, several times a week. It is important, particularly for at-risk readers, to determine an appropriate level of text difficulty. These children need to start with texts where they will be assured of success and move up gradually. Before reading aloud they can practise by taping their readings, listening to it with their partner, and talking about how to improve it. Only when they're satisfied with their reading should they present it to an audience.

18. An at-risk reader can be a buddy reader to a younger child. The older child finds a book to read during the buddy session and practises it before reading it aloud to the younger child. The opportunity to read to another who will see them as a reader serves as a confidence builder.

19. Buddy reading, where a fluent and weaker reader read together, was originally intended to be practised between a child and parent. In paired reading, the child and fluent reader read together, with the fluent reader taking the lead. If desired, the child can signal that she or he wants to read alone or with only minimal input from the partner. When the child has trouble, the fluent reader can step in.

20. For some children, having a tape of the story gives them the confidence to read it. Although there are a number of commercial tapes, a child can benefit from hearing your voice. You can read the text word by word at a rate that is comfortable for the child. When the child can read the text fluently, she or he can tape the story for another reader. While the focus of the activity is reading for pleasure, rereading aids fluency, and increases sight vocabulary and story comprehension.

An Example of Intervention – Reading Recovery®

Sometimes, a child requires specialized help, and this process is significant to the child's future success as a reader. Whether the program is inclusive or is based on withdrawal, you will need to be aware of the support your community can offer in assisting young readers in difficulty.

For example, Reading Recovery® was developed by Dame Marie Clay to help young readers in grades one and two. Its premise is simple – withdraw children who are experiencing serious reading delays and have them work with a specially trained teacher on a one-to-one basis for a 30-minute period each day. When the child is at a level that is similar to that of the majority of his or her peers, she or he no longer needs the program and can return to the regular program.

The program began in New Zealand and is gaining in popularity in North America. Assessment of children is one of its cornerstones – children need to be assessed and a thorough understanding of their abilities and knowledge determined before the program begins. Each child's program is unique and builds on what the child knows. Only those children who are considered seriously at risk are eligible for the program.

Reading recovery teachers have special training in reading development. The program that the teacher draws up for each child is centred on using children's books and the child's own stories as the basis for learning. By drawing the child's attention to sound-letter correspondences and letter patterns, the teacher can help the child to explore the connections between oral language and print. A reading recovery session may include the following components:

- reading a new story,
- making words using magnetic letters,
- writing a story together,
- talking about the story,
- analyzing words and patterns in the story,
- rereading a story that was read the previous day to allow the teacher to note progress.

36: Teacher Demonstrations and Mini-Lessons

All of us learn from the demonstrations of others: we learned how to ride a bicycle by watching others ride. We may have learned to use a computer by following the demonstrations of a proficient user. We will continue to learn from the demonstrations of others throughout our lives.

Demonstrations give us concrete examples of a concept we need to learn, a strategy we need to practise, or knowledge we need to acquire.

As teachers, when we model how we read – by thinking aloud and sharing our strategies – we demonstrate for children aspects of the reading process and the inquiry process. If we demonstrate a behavior or strategy repeatedly, we help children to understand the concept on a deeper level – a level that will allow them to take on the strategy or knowledge as their own.

Demonstrations can happen at any time during the school day. They are conscious, explicit attempts to show children how something is done. They can be spontaneous (e.g., the outcome of a conference with a child), or planned (e.g., when we see a child struggle with a concept that can be made more explicit). They can be done in a range of situations – on an individual basis, with a small group, or with the class. Demonstrations can have a powerful and lasting effect on the learner, but it is the implicit aspect that explains their richness and importance. Classrooms need to be filled with relevant and functional literacy demonstrations.

To strengthen our impact, we need to demonstrate the concept or strategy repeatedly, model a variety of events, ensure that necessary resources are available to the children, and observe the children to assess their growth. As well, we need to keep in mind that our demonstrations must help children learn. They must be manageable, informative, and applicable to the child's stage of development.

As parents and teachers, we model behaviors we want children to adopt. An important component of literacy is the opportunity to see reading behaviors modelled in the home and at school. When children see that their parents, older siblings, and teachers read novels, newspapers, and non-fiction texts, they see the value and satisfaction that comes from reading. Teachers can unknowingly give negative demonstrations to children in a variety of ways: reading is a serious business; there is one interpretation—the teacher's; children are not smart enough to choose their own texts; reading is always followed by a test; teachers talk a lot about literature, but they don't read much of it; reading is a waste of class time. In contrast, how often do children see their teacher captivated by what they are reading and making evident to them the processes involved?

Elements of Successful Demonstrations

1. Explicit demonstrations need to be demonstrations of language "wholes" (i.e., all the pieces must fit) rather than isolated, unrelated bits of language.
2. Demonstrations need to be continually repeated. Since demonstrations are larger, more general, and more contextual than mini-lessons, children can learn something new again and again from a similar demonstration.
3. There is no set length for a demonstration. Children will generally take from a demonstration whatever they find interesting or relevant to their learning needs.
4. Demonstrations should be contextually relevant and therefore appropriate to the literacy task the child is trying to complete. Children will engage with a demonstration if they have a need for what you are showing them.
5. Part of an ongoing series of demonstrations are the reading expectations you have of your students. You need to expect them to read, to discover books they love, to find satisfaction in books, and to learn from them.
6. Know enough about reading literacy to be able to present a range and variety of demonstrations that will enable learners to get all the pieces they need to become fully literate.
7. Demonstrations are more effective when delivered to smaller groups.
8. A good form of demonstration is the "think-aloud" process you can demonstrate as you read a shared text aloud to them. Reading the text and then reflecting out loud on what you have read shows children that adults also need support and time to reflect, revealing a variety of strategies and different ways to approach a text.
9. Encourage children to use the methods and habits used by good readers, so they will become self-monitoring and independent, and able to read with depth and meaning.
10. Following a demonstration, children need the opportunity to practise their learning.

Mini-Lessons

A mini-lesson is a brief, focused lesson that allows teachers to demonstrate or teach a specific skill or idea in a short, purposeful way. Reading, writing, or thinking strategies can all be demonstrated using mini-lessons, which are often generated by the needs of the children. As well, mini-lessons can be used to review classroom procedures, to show ways to think about what has been read, and to teach specific reading strategies.

A good, powerful mini-lesson should be short (approximately 10 minutes), specific, and relevant to what children are doing so that it will "stick" (particularly if they can put to use immediately the skill or strategy). The question-answer method should be avoided when giving mini-lessons as it can slow the lesson and detract from teaching the skill or concept. Instead, children can save their questions for the end where questions asked can be indicators of children's depth of understanding of the concept.

Introduce the concept of mini-lessons early in the year by letting the children know the behavior expected of them (e.g., where do they meet for mini-lessons?). Keep in mind that content mini-lessons are most effective when delivered to small groups of children or an individual child. For mini-lessons dealing with topics that children will refer to repeatedly (e.g., punctuation), teach the mini-lesson using chart paper. When completed, it can be hung together with related charts and displayed on the walls for children's reference.

Topics for Mini-Lessons

- a phonic generalization
- strategies effective readers use
- suggestions for writing journals
- characteristics of an author's works
- characteristics of a genre
- how to read a poem
- how to read a short story
- examples of an opening chapter or opening sentences
- different writing styles of authors
- exploring elements of novels – characters, plot, setting, theme, time, mood – and literary devices
- noticing point of view
- examples of narrative voice, dialogue
- prologues, epilogues, sequels
- rhythm/sound, rhyme, imagery, or sequence

- reading aloud, reading for speed, skimming, or scanning
- rereading or abandoning a book
- how to select good books
- how to rate books for peers
- how to keep a reading journal
- why we need to talk about books after reading
- how to talk about what you read with a teacher, or with peers
- how books are published
- how to organize in groups
- timetables regarding the use of classroom computers
- use of resources in the class and library (e.g., dictionaries, writing handbooks)
- daily class routines
- goals in reading and writing
- how to assess reading growth
- how to assess participation in literature circles, discussion groups
- procedures to follow in group conferences

37: Conducting Conferences

Conferences are essential in developing "a community of readers and writers" and should be a part of each school day. While there are several types of conferences, and each has its own structure and purpose, all conferences share the same general goals:
- to relate language learning to the child's life experiences,
- to improve the child's attitude toward reading and writing,
- to assess a child's reading and writing either privately or in small groups and to offer helpful, needed assistance,
- to share personal interests in reading texts,
- to build strategies for word recognition and comprehension,
- to develop oral reading competence,
- to introduce new books to groups of children,
- to model ways to talk about books,
- to help a child build understanding through conversation,
- to deepen a reading experience with extending discussion,
- to provide a forum for questioning,
- to help the child venture forth into new learning with more complex materials,

- to help build the child's self-confidence,
- to build a literacy community incorporating children at all levels of development.

Types of Conferences

Child-Teacher Conferences
Through the use of child-teacher conferences, we can encourage children to extend their exploration of a text, and we can assess and evaluate their progress. In addition, our support during the conference helps to promote the sharing aspect of reading and encourages children to feel that they are a member of a literacy community.

These conferences give children varied and frequent opportunities to talk about books they have read. The conferences should take place in a relaxed atmosphere where the children feel secure and comfortable in expressing their feelings about what they have read. During these conferences, we can:
- listen to children talk about interests, attitudes, and purposes for reading,
- ask questions to promote their exploration of the text,
- identify reading strategies the children use,
- foster the use of more efficient strategies,
- determine the children's comprehension of what they have read,
- expand on children's oral reading fluency,
- activate the children's thinking,
- recommend other books on a similar theme,
- draw children's attention to books that present contrasting themes or views,
- recommend other books by the same author,
- promote related forms of writing,
- suggest further response activities (e.g., drama),
- advocate further research,
- encourage the children's own writing,
- assess children's reading competence.

Peer Conferences
This form of conference requires a learning climate that is friendly and open, and that emphasizes the importance of peer interaction. For us, it offers a way to integrate learning with assessment. In this conference, we need to:
- organize small groups,
- begin lists of questions children can refer to as needed,
- encourage children to tell and retell,

- promote relating and reflecting as part of the group's experiences,
- help children obtain feedback on their progress.

Parent-Child-Teacher Conference
The third type of conference – parent-child-teacher – promotes children's reading at home. Each party has responsibilities in this conference.

Parents can:
- encourage reading at home,
- ensure that the child has a private time and place to read,
- share reading and understanding of books they have read,
- support reading growth,
- offer helpful suggestions.

Children can:
- share their response to the book, ask questions, and demonstrate understanding,
- read aloud or retell parts of the book to their teacher and parents.

We can:
- encourage reading at home,
- maintain teacher-parent communication,
- extend the community of readers by sharing books with parents and family,
- show that assessment and evaluation are integral parts of learning.

Elements of Conferences
1. Children should feel comfortable. They know that their ideas and opinions will be respected.
2. Physical comfort is also a factor. The conference space can be held in a private corner, or on a rug made comfortable with pillows. Conference areas should be well-stocked with paper and writing materials.
3. Children should have the opportunity to record elements of the conference (e.g., a suggestion they want to remember). They can record notes on special conference sheets or use a special pen that is used only for conferences. As well, conferences can be recorded. If recording is not an option, we can make jot notes that can be transcribed and added to when time allows.
4. Open-ended questions, as opposed to specific comments, are more helpful to the children's work and self-esteem, and lead to more reflective self-assessment.

---

5. Descriptive, non-judgmental phrases, suggestions, and support are necessary for the confidence that each child needs in order to develop his or her reading abilities.
6. Conferences can be available on an as-needed basis. A sign-up sheet listing stages and children's names can be completed by children so that you can meet at least several times throughout the project. Children who require a conference immediately can add a star beside their name.
7. The main point of a conference is to allow children the chance to talk – to retell their reading experiences, to problem solve, and to celebrate. While our input is valuable in a conference, it should not dominate it.
8. In order to improve a conference, we can ask ourselves these questions: How am I benefiting or learning from this conference? How can I grow? What new or different resources might be helpful? What new book can I read now? Will taping and analyzing a conference help? When is a good opportunity to do this? Such questions result in our growth, which in turn results in the growth of a child.
9. Since it is not always possible to have long conferences with everyone, we can mix short and long conferences. Some children may be at a stage when more discussion is necessary, others may not. Conference length can be changed according to time, stages of reading, and the needs of the participants.
10. A child who is unable to focus on his or her own work may act as a recorder for other children's conferences. This makes the child feel worthwhile, and she or he may gain from repeated exposures to conferences and positive attitudes toward reading and writing.

38: Skimming and Scanning

Skimming and scanning are useful reading strategies children can use when reading for information, when rereading a text, or when deciding whether to read a text. When we skim a text, we form a general picture of it, and have a sense of the main ideas covered in the text. When we scan a text, we look for the answer to a specific question. You can discuss with the children how, in these situations, we do not read every word. Instead, we employ a strategy where we skim through a text looking for key words, and focus on headings and opening and end paragraphs.

One way to introduce this strategy to children is to provide them with a list of questions and a text that answers the questions. Children review the questions, then skim the text for answers. Set a time limit for the activity so children know they do not have time to read the entire text. As a tip, include key words from the questions in the text.

Another method is to have the children skim a text and make predictions about what the text is about. Children list their predictions, then compare them with those of a partner. Children then read the text to see how their predictions compare to the content of the text. Playing games with used phone books or with dictionaries can demonstrate the need for quickly skimming text and scanning to find a name or a word. For example, children need to skim the text to find the first letters of the last name, and they need to scan it to find the name.

39: Cloze Procedures

Cloze procedures involve oral or written deletions of parts of words, whole words, or phrases in a passage of text. "Clozing," or restoring these gaps, requires children to scan the text, recognize and process contextual cues, and then choose the most appropriate word. The reader learns to use context to help figure out unfamiliar words. It's an active, constructive language process.

Cloze activities are suitable for use at all grade levels and help to build a number of skills exhibited by strong, fluent readers:

- they focus on contextual cueing systems, strengthening the readers' abilities to anticipate the text to make the most sense,
- children interact with text – searching, scanning, and thinking – that may result in making meaning with print. Cloze can help expand the readers' repertoires of thinking strategies,
- the readers' confidence increases – as they experience success with cloze, readers realize that they can predict in order to recognize words.
- they are useful for assessing children's reading ability, comprehension, and vocabulary awareness.

Using Cloze Activities

Before preparing a cloze activity, we need to identify objectives:

1. Cloze activities should have a collaborative component where children can brainstorm, discuss, and debate responses, focus on problem-solving skills, and share and value contributions.
2. Cloze activities can help emergent readers develop reading fluency by encouraging them to move from letter recognition to word recognition as they interact with text, focusing on context and meaning, predicting and confirming as they meet new words.
3. Cloze activities encourage readers who rely on memory to focus more on print. We can sometimes help them predict a word by supplying its initial letter.
4. Cloze activities encourage readers who rely on print to focus on meaning when content words such as nouns and verbs are deleted.
5. Oral cloze activities encourage the development of listening and comprehension skills, focusing on semantic and syntactic cues.
6. Cloze activities can focus on language structure (i.e., syntactic cues) when structure words such as articles and pronouns are deleted.
7. Cloze activities explore elements of genre when they focus on genre-specific forms (e.g., rhythm and rhyme in lyrics or poems).
8. Cloze activities expand or review vocabulary when the children are provided with a definition of the missing word.
9. Cloze activities strengthen sight vocabulary, pronunciation, and spelling when they focus on patterns in words and word families.
10. Cloze activities stimulate children's creative writing when they involve deleted sentences or paragraphs.

Selecting a Text for Cloze Procedures

Cloze procedures help us to assess the appropriate level of reading material, and can help to reveal a child's understanding of what is being read. While any type of text can be used for a cloze exercise (e.g., familiar and unfamiliar stories, letters, instructions, comic strips, poems, riddles, songs, articles, diary entries, recipes, advertisements, interviews), it is important that the text be well written. In this way, children are predicting supported by the contexts found in quality writing.

- Choose a text children can read independently when presented as intact.
- Choose a familiar text to introduce young children to cloze.
- Motivate children by using a text that interests them.
- Choose a text that reflects children's objectives (e.g., recalling a story, reviewing a specific form of text).
- Consider the teaching strategy (e.g., rhyming text is effective as oral cloze).

Designing a Cloze Activity

1. Deletions can target particular words or can be made arbitrarily by formula (e.g., every fifth word). Cloze exercises can also be tailored by
   - deleting parts of words, whole words, or phrases, retaining words that are structurally interdependent,
   - providing visual aids (e.g., the first letter of each deleted word) when introducing written cloze to young children,
   - using dashes, boxes, or numbers in brackets to indicate the number of letters deleted.
2. Along with the choice of text and children's knowledge and literacy levels, the deletions we make will strongly influence the difficulty of a cloze activity. We need to consider that:
   - content words such as nouns and verbs are more difficult to predict than structure words such as articles,
   - deletions at the beginning of a sentence are more difficult to predict than those made at its middle or end,
   - difficulty increases with the number of deletions made.
3. To maximize the learning benefits of cloze activities, we can structure a lesson to focus on the process of restoring deletions as opposed to the end product. In pairs, small groups, or as a class, children generate, discuss, debate, justify, compare, and select possible solutions for each deletion. The author's original choice is only useful when presented as a focus for discussion: Why might the author have chosen this word or phrase?
4. Independent activity worksheets may not capitalize on the potential for learning. Given the range of experience and literacy skills of a group of children, individual cloze will be boring for

some and frustrating for others. Teachers can combine independent cloze work with group discussion, and group children with varying abilities.

5. Written cloze can be presented in a variety of ways. An enlarged reproduction can be prepared for a whole-class activity. Pairs or groups can use worksheets before gathering as a class to share, compare, and discuss selections.
6. For oral cloze, we can read aloud and pause at deletions so children can brainstorm, record, and discuss predictions. Illustrations can be used as visual cues. Many of us present oral cloze regularly – predicting what will happen next in a story is cloze.
7. Children can ask themselves these questions when attempting to select words:
   - What is this text about?
   - What kind of text is this?
   - What is the author trying to say?
   - How is the author trying to say it?
   - Why does this make sense?
   - Is that the way we would say it?
   - Why would that word work?
   - What other words could we use?

Examples of Cloze Activities

1. Create a rhyme cloze by deleting rhyming words in a passage of text.
2. Prepare a homophone cloze, for example: "I was___tired___read the last___pages."
3. An example of a grammar cloze would show all adjectives deleted; another, all adverbs.
4. Replace deletions with pictures in a rebus cloze.
5. Create a "Wheel of Fortune" cloze to illustrate to children how consonants, vowels, and first, last, and middle letters help us identify words.
6. Prepare a vowel hunt by deleting the same vowel throughout the text. You can also do this with a consonant, prefix, suffix, phoneme, syllable, letter string, or word.
7. Replace each deletion with its definition.
8. Provide alternatives for each deletion or a general word selection list.
9. Replace deletions with nonsensical words to make nonsense clozes.
10. Use a familiar passage to make a missing cloze. Provide the first letter of every word. Successively add one letter at a time to each word until the text is decipherable.

40: Think Alouds

When we ask a child to think aloud, or when a child thinks aloud as she or he solves a problem, we can witness, at least in part, their thinking processes as they work:

1. Before we ask a child to think aloud, we have to establish a climate of trust since it can be unnerving to describe to another what we are thinking and children are no different in this regard.
2. Once such an environment is established, we can begin to ask children to tell us what they are thinking. A natural time to ask is when we see a child stumble while reading.
3. When listening to the child describe his or her thought processes, we need to refrain from asking leading questions for children may assume that we are looking for a particular response.
4. When children have finished describing the process, we can discuss how this particular strategy helps them to problem solve.
5. Articulating the process helps the children to become aware of strategies they have on hand and empowers them as readers because they begin to realize they have ways to learn that they can call on when needed.
6. We can extend their learning by modelling aloud our own "think aloud" strategies as a demonstration. Reading is a strategy-based activity; when children are aware of the strategies they need to read, they are more confident in their ability to tackle new text.

41: Storytelling to and with Children

Children like to listen to a well-told story – they see the stories in their mind and are free to interpret details based on their experiences. While storytelling can be an intimidating event for those of us who feel more comfortable holding a book, we need to experiment with the genre so that we can offer children another form of story. The children can tell stories to one another and share in an art form that has been practised for centuries.

The following activities acquaint children with the process of storytelling and can help them to explore the genre.

1. Retelling the Story as Part of a Large Group
Read the title of the text to the children. Ask them to predict the genre of the text based on its title, as well as the type of writing (factual, narrative) and possible words and phrases that may be included in the text. List their predictions. Read the text to the children, or have the children read the text. Children can then check for predictions listed earlier. When all children have finished, ask them to suggest how they can retell the text orally as a large group. Children retell the story and reread the original text before comparing the two. Discuss, as a large group, details they omitted or changed in their story.

2. Telling a Folktale to a Group
Find a folktale that is unfamiliar to the class and share it with one child. She or he prepares and presents a storytelling session to the rest of the class. Children then read the folktale. When everyone has finished, children can discuss the story they heard and the story they read.

3. Telling a Favorite Story
Children choose their favorite story. They note its essential points, then create a retelling, which they share with a partner.

4. In Role
After telling a story to the children, ask them to form groups. Each group can then divide the roles of the characters in the story, and rework the story (keeping essential elements intact). After practising their version of the story, children present their work to other groups.

42: Talking About Books

The reading experiences of children can be extended by what others reveal to them about their reading, and what they reveal to others about their reading. Text-based discussions in the classroom give children the opportunity to construct meaning from the text by returning to it to clarify and modify their ideas. Giving children the means to engage in discussion about a text gives them the power to edit and reform their perceptions, as well as to expand personal meaning and deepen comprehension.

In *Booktalk*, Aidan Chambers has provided a series of sample questions of an open-ended nature that contribute to lively interchanges of meanings among children. Although the list in the book is extensive, Chambers once stated in a workshop that the following four questions would stimulate any discussion you could hope to have with a child.
1. Tell me about the parts you liked the most.
2. Tell me about the parts you didn't like.
3. Was there anything that puzzled you?
4. Did you notice anything in the story or poem that made a pattern?

How to Get Children to Talk About Their Reading

Before children can start talking, they may need a goal or point for discussion. We can provide them with these points by implementing the following steps:

1. Letting Individuals Prepare for Discussion
Children need time to reflect on a text and formulate their ideas before they discuss them with others. We can encourage them to record their responses to a text in their journals as a preparatory step to discussing them in peer and group situations. The act of recording a response may increase children's comfort level at later stages when sharing their ideas.

2. Discussing with a Partner
Children can share their thoughts and ideas about a text with a partner. They can use their journal responses from the previous step to support the discussion if they wish.

3. Discussing as Part of a Small Group
In groups of four, children can discuss ideas and modify and deepen their thinking. This text talk is the essence of revealing and extending comprehension.

4. Sharing as Part of a Large Group
Depending on the nature of the discussion, ideas stemming from small-group discussions can be shared among classmates. This form of sharing can be done by jigsaw grouping where each child, in his or her small group, takes a number from one to four. Children from other groups who also took that number form a second group. New group members take turns sharing their previous group's discussion.

5. Book Clubs
Have the children meet on a regular basis (e.g., weekly, monthly) in groups to discuss books they have read. The book clubs can be organized according to various genres: for example, fiction, non-fiction, poetry, science fiction, and mystery.

6. Book Recommendations
Children take turns to recommend a book to the rest of the class or other classes in the school. A class poster can be created that displays their recommendations and ratings. Children can decide and vote on favorite categories.

7. A One-Minute Book Talk
Children can select a book they have read. In a one-minute time period, they share their opinion of the book in a small- or large-group situation.

8. Share Time
Provide a daily time for children to share thoughts about a book they have read with the rest of the class. Keep a record of sharing times in order to ensure that each child has opportunities to share his or her reading.

9. Debates
Select a book that the class has read and make a statement about it. Divide the class into two, or select volunteers to form two debating groups. One group argues for the statement while the other group argues against it. Prior to beginning the debate, the children can be briefed on debating rules. Choose one child to be the chairperson. At the end of the debate, children can complete a checklist to help them determine which team provided the soundest argument. The criteria for the checklist can include the following factors: planned as a team, made a team effort, kept to time limit, spoke clearly, and provided a good summary.

10. A Thirty-Second Radio Spot
The children can prepare and tape record a thirty-second advertisement that recommends a book they have read and that they think others would enjoy. These advertisements can be prepared for other classes in the school, based on individual and class responses to books. Advertisements could be taped and played over the school's public-address system.

43: Prompts for Responding to Books

These prompts can be grouped for a particular emphasis, or posted for children to select from when they are writing in their journals or when preparing for a literature discussion.

- What were your expectations when you began reading this book?
- Did you change your mind as you got into the book?
- What puzzles grew out of reading this book?
- What did you learn about life from the book, about different places, about history, science, religion, etc.?
- Did the author have enough background about the content of the book to help you learn more as a reader?
- How fast did the author move the plot along?
- Who was the voice the author chose as narrator – first person, third person, a storyteller, an anonymous voice, a different voice, or the author himself or herself? Did this style work well?
- Did the sequence of events in the story appear as they were happening, or was the story told as if it had happened some time before?
- Does the story unfold over a long period of time, or is it told over a matter of days?
- Did you find out about events in the order in which they would actually have happened?
- Were there any plot shifts in time, space-flashforwards or flashbacks, or two stories being told at the same time?
- What events in the story were not actually written, but you understood from between the lines what was happening?
- If you were the author, would you change the order of any of the events?
- Did you hope an event in the book would not happen, but it happened anyway?
- Did anything happen to you just as it happened in the story?
- When were you first held hostage by the story and knew that you had to finish it, no matter what?
- What were the main issues or problems that the plot revolved around?
- Were there twists and turns in the story that surprised you?
- What was the mood or atmosphere of the story, or did it change as you read the book? What music would you tell a friend to play if they were preparing to read the book?
- Did you wonder what might happen next? Were there any clues about was going to happen? Was it too easy to predict the events of the plot? Was the plot not important to the fun of the story?
- Was the ending of the book what you had expected, or were there surprises?
- What writing techniques did the author use to build to the ending? Would you have liked another ending?
- Whose story could you say the book is really telling?
- What was more important – the plot or the characters?
- Was the author able to involve you emotionally in the story? Did you laugh or cry?
- Did you ever feel that you were actually in the story being told, or did you feel as if you were a spectator or an eavesdropper?
- Do you think characters in life would act as they did in the story?
- Should the characters have been more life-like?
- Which character in the book did you connect with? Do you know why?
- Would the story have been different if that character had been omitted?
- Which character did you dislike? Were you ever frustrated by one of the characters? Which character would you like to become?
- How did the author help us to know what the characters were thinking?
- Were there any characters who were not described at length but who could have been important to the story?
- Were you able to see the events of the story through the eyes of the characters?
- What would you have done if you were inside the book and you could have helped one of the characters?
- Did the characters remind you of other personalities in television or films?
- Was the dialogue realistic? Could you hear people in life saying those words?
- Did you know enough about the characters from reading the book to believe in them as if they actually existed? Would you like to know any of them?

- Did the setting of the story help you to understand the characters; how did the author create a place that seems real?
- Did the author use description well? Was there enough or too much?
- What did you notice about the style of the writing? How did the book begin – with a question, dialogue, a shocking statement, one word? How did each chapter begin?
- Were there long sentences? Short choppy ones?
- Was there a common trick or convention the author used throughout the book? Did you notice any in-jokes?
- Were there examples of slang, different spellings, or strange words or expressions that the author used for a reason?
- What special images do you remember from the story?
- Has the book become a movie? Would the story work well on film?
- Was the design of the cover or the book jacket effective? Did it catch your attention?
- If there were illustrations, how did they add to the value of the book?
- Was the blurb on the back useful?
- Was the book the right length – too short or too long? How were the chapters organized – long or short? Was the book divided into sections?
- How did others who read the book feel? Do you understand your own responses to the characters and the story?
- In your conversations and responses to the story, were you able to change or affect any of your classmates' ideas or opinions about the book?
- What about this book did you especially like? What do you wish there were more of in the story?
- Did you have any difficulties with the book? How did you handle them?
- Have you read this book before? Was the second reading different?
- Did you read the book at one sitting, or a chapter at a time?
- If you had written the book, how would you have changed it?
- Did this book make you think about your own life in a different way?
- Has it influenced what you think? What you believe in? Your view of the world?
- Have you learned anything about yourself or others from reading this book?

- What passages from the book do you especially remember?
- What quotations would you choose from this book to make a poster for your bedroom wall?
- Would you recommend this book to a younger reader?
- Why do you think the author wrote this book?
- Do you know other writings by this author? A series? A sequel? An autobiography? A picture book? Have you read any of them? Can you find patterns in the things the author writes about, in the events of the stories, in the characters, in the ideas the author seems to believe in, in the style of the writing?
- Have you read any information about the author, or seen a videotape of the author speaking?
- Has the author used his her own life in creating the story?
- What type of research went into the writing of this book?
- Have you read comments about the author's works, such as reviews or opinions from classmates? Do you know what the author is working on now?
- Are there books similiar to those of this author that you have read?
- Did you choose to read this author because of the type of story she or he writes, or because of the content of the story?
- What questions would you ask the author about the book or about his or her life?

44: Questions that Matter

In past decades, children were often required to prove their mastery of curriculum content by answering teacher-generated questions, most of which demanded brief, factual responses. This method of teaching often encouraged children to memorize answers, but did little to foster indepth inquiry, a necessary component of deeply structured learning. As educators extended their understanding of how children learn, they began to modify their questioning techniques. We now know that open-ended questions can serve a variety of functions, including introducing reading tasks by stimulating interest and curiosity, setting up problems that require reading, identifying important ideas to look for when reading, reinforcing and organizing ideas gained from reading, and helping readers to construct meaning and initiate dialogue.

We ask questions that help children to develop higher-order thinking skills and that require them to draw on personal knowledge and experience. We foster environments that are conducive to sharing ideas and opinions, realizing that the environment in which questions are asked is as important as the questions. For many of us, a natural outgrowth of this approach is the development of child-generated questions as an integral part of the classroom climate.

Children as Questioners

We know that for true learning to occur, children need to be able to pose questions. When children ask questions about a story, they require a detailed knowledge of the text and need to have thought deeply about what they've read. The ability to interrogate the text has application in all areas of life, and has particular relevance to tasks such as problem solving. Children can increase their questioning powers by drawing from the models that we present, but we can also teach questioning as a process. The following activities allow children to learn about questioning and may help them to overcome any discomfort they may experience when asking questions.

Tips for Asking Good Questions

1. Avoid asking yes/no questions. Instead, ask open-ended questions.
2. Avoid repeating children's responses since this encourages them to listen to you and not to one another. Arrange the children so that they can hear and see one another.
3. Use probing techniques to help children move beyond their original response (e.g., "How does that relate to...?").
4. Be prepared to change the order of questions if a discussion takes an unexpected, fruitful turn.
5. Be aware of the intent of your questions. Questions can elicit information, shape understanding, or press for reflection. It is important to ask a variety of questions as all have value.
6. Questions require a wait time – the time a respondent needs to consider a question and formulate an answer. As well, it is important to pause after the response is given. This provides an opportunity for the respondent to modify or elaborate on his or her response and for others to read and add their ideas.

Activities that Promote Effective Questioning

1. Question/Question
Children find a partner. In pairs, they practise asking questions by answering each question with another question. For example:
A: Are we going together?
B: Do you want me to come with you?
A: Isn't it necessary for both of us to go?
B: How much do we have to carry?

2. Answer/Question
Present children with an answer (statements from a familiar text) and have them provide the question. This is an effective means of testing children's knowledge and understanding.

3. Re-Quest
In Re-Quest, or Reciprocal Questioning, you and the children take turns asking one another questions about a small segment of a text. Begin by reading a sentence from the text. Close the book and answer questions the children ask about the sentence. Reverse roles. Children read a sentence, close their books, and answer questions you ask. The activity can also include silent reading of a short passage. Children ask you questions about the reading; you answer and then pose questions to them. This is a good opportunity to model how to ask and answer questions by drawing on information in the text and existing knowledge.

4. Role-Play
Role-playing offers children another way to question curriculum content. As an example, a child in the role of a novel character can be questioned by another child in the role of a reporter.

5. Brainstorming
Select an informational text and give the class a brief overview of one topic outlined in it. Children then find a partner and generate, within a ten- to fifteen-minute time period, questions that may be answered about the topic in the text. When the time limit is up, children take turns calling out their questions. You can record their responses on chart paper then read the section of the text that pertains to the topic. Children compare the information in the text with the questions they generated: which questions were/were not answered in the text? Which aspects were not addressed by questions? List any new questions that can lead to further reading and research.

45: Oral Reading

In a traditional reading lesson, children read aloud so that we could check pronunciation and reading fluency. Naturally, this was a difficult time for children who were having difficulty reading and it wasn't particularly useful for other children listening in the class. Today's children have time and opportunity to understand and practise a story before they share it orally.

Oral reading, when handled properly, can help children to strengthen their understanding of a story. When they read aloud parts they have rehearsed to a partner, or as members of a small group, many children find it a pleasant way to experience the story. In addition to reading for enjoyment, children can take part in oral reading to find answers to questions, to read in preparation for dramatization, and to illustrate specific details from the text that support their opinion. Shared reading of big books or choral reading of a poem can help to bolster children's confidence, particularly those who are at risk or are learning a second language.

Reasons for Oral Reading
1. Experience poems and rhymes, saying them in the comfort offered by the group.
2. Read big books and favorite lines from familiar texts.
3. Read personal, published writing to others.
4. Read to prove a discussion point.
5. Read material on a topic of interest to other children.
6. Practice for dramatizations of text.
7. Respond to text, by chanting or singing lines.
8. Share parts of texts that they found moving or reflective of a theme.

46: Choral Reading

Choral reading, similar to paired reading, is done as a group, offering readers a safe venue in which to practise reading. After several sessions, most children, including those at-risk, can usually read passages fluently, giving children a sense of accomplishment.

Children benefit from choral reading by developing:
- concentation skills,
- memory skills,
- a sense of security and unity,
- group solidarity,
- social skills,
- trust in groups
- intonation, rhythm, and beat,
- visual and auditory memory,
- reading fluency.

Getting Started

Younger children need to be taught choral reading using a simple rote process. Short, lively nursery rhymes work well.
1. Read the selection to the children.
2. Reread the poem and discuss the words with the children. Is the poem funny, mysterious, calming?
3. Read it again and ask the children to join in on specific parts or words of the poem.
4. The children join in as much as they can each time you read the poem.
5. Lessen the amount you read aloud until the children are reading alone.

Even young children can handle relatively sophisticated material. The success of the activity depends on our interests and skills. Older children enjoy reading a variety of texts chorally – poems, songs, scripts, chants, cheers, prayers.

47: Drama and Reading

Drama is an outgrowth of dramatic play with young children. Their play can be guided and encouraged in a variety of ways: play centres can be transformed into settings that provoke role-playing around a chosen theme or issue. Props can be used in a variety of ways to stimulate role-play. We can observe the children at spontaneous play and learn about their concerns, interests, and anxieties. Dramatic games can help to promote a positive class climate where children can expect to be listened to and have their contributions valued.

To begin drama work, we can elicit simple dialogue – questions in role. We can ask children to respond as if they are a character in a book we are reading aloud. Gradually, children can move into speculations based on what they imagine. Keeping children in a circle is a good initial management technique that provides perimeters for the activity and supports all children as equal participants. We can devise a signal to indicate when work will begin or end. Children can work in pairs, in small groups, or as a large group; the more children can be actively involved at any one time, the better. When possible, role-playing can begin as a whole-class activity, move into small group and individual work situations, and end with a whole-group situation.

Time Considerations

A drama workshop can last for one session or many, depending on the interest of the children and the possibilities inherent in the themes or materials with which the group is working. We can extend a unit through linking dramatizations that take place in different times or places, or under different conditions.

We can collectively decide when the drama is over, based on our satisfaction with the outcome of events. Often, we will try to keep the children from rushing to a resolution of a problem in drama by challenging superficial responses, pressing for elaboration, and deepening simplistic contributions. Belief and commitment in drama on our part passes on to children the importance and power of words and language.

Drama is a shared learning experience and col-laborative group effort – the threads of individual response are woven together to build an improvised world in which all children share. Drama reveals and provides skills for negotiating problems of classroom dynamics and interpersonal relationships. It can enhance individual and group self-esteem – children with learning exceptionalities often experience great success with drama. As we make sense of others' stories, we come closer to understanding our own.

Drama Activities

1. Familiar Stories
An easy way to begin is to have children form small groups to dramatize familiar stories using their own words. When children have dramatized the story, they can explore events that might have taken place before or after the story, changing aspects of date, mood, and locale.

2. Special Effects
Integrate the visual arts and music with drama by having children make masks and puppets to be used in dramatizations. Simple, improvised orchestration or sound effects can be created by the children to accompany or punctuate drama. The playing of music can set the tone for their work.

3. Movement
Mime and movement can help children build a repertoire of body movements. Using literature that has an action orientation, children can take turns reading or narrating the selection and miming the actions described in it. They can also work in groups to mime the actions of the tale.

4. Interviews
Interviews provide an opportunity to plan questions related to a text's author or illustrator, or a character from the text. Prior to planning and role-playing interviews, you can introduce children to interview structures and the types of questioning techniques that elicit responses.

After the Drama

Children need a chance to explain and analyze their actions and decisions. This form of reflection, discussion, and writing makes conscious the learning that took place during the drama. It is often useful to have a large-group discussion about everyone's role.

48: Reading Response Journals

Reading response journals contain children's ideas, reactions, and opinions of what they have read. They are a way for children to organize their thoughts and to record ideas generated by the story. When we respond to children's journals, we can comment on their ideas, perhaps making connections between experiences and encouraging them to explore other aspects of their reading. Journals can also be discussed during conferences to add insight into a child's reading.

When children first use a journal, many simply retell what they have read. As their familiarity grows and their confidence in themselves as readers develops, children begin to use the journal as a sounding board for their perceptions and reactions. We need to encourage children to write in their journals regularly. Their entries can take many forms, including point-form notes, webs, illustrations, and notes to us.

Our purpose in reading their journals is to discover what the children are thinking about in their reading, to help them develop strategies that will enable them to develop as readers, and to focus on making meaning. If our goal is to have children extend their thinking and learning, then we need be genuine in our comments. We can dialogue with the child about his or her thoughts as recorded in the journal, recording our own responses to the book and commenting on the child's reflective comments. Often the child and the teacher write their responses as letters to each other. This format allows us to deepen the child's thoughts, helps extend their ideas, moves into personal experiences, focuses on interpretive skills, or redirects a reader who has been sidetracked or confused.

The following example of excerpts by the child and the teacher centres around a child's experience with *Number the Stars* by Lois Lowry.

Dear Mr. Swartz,

I chose the book Number the Stars to read because it won an award and because it's about the war. It looks a little bit too hard for me to read. If I finish it, it will be the longest book I read this year. Joanna is my partner. I'll try and keep up with her.

Last night when I told my mom about the book, she told me a story about the war. She was separated from her family and went to live with some rich people. Her seven sisters had to go to school in another town. When the war was over, she got back with her mom and dad. Her uncle was killed in the war. I think I'm going to like Number the Stars because it's about a girl (older than me) who has to survive during the war. I think she's Jewish because on the cover she wore a necklace.

Laura

Laura,

I hope you're enjoying Number the Stars. If it gets too difficult in parts maybe Joanna can help you. (I can too!) Good for you for giving it a try.

The necklace on the front cover is a star of David. It's a symbol of the Jewish faith. I used to have a necklace with that star, but the chain broke and I lost it.

I'm interested in your family's story about the war. I'm sure many people in our class have stories about families who fought or survived in the war. When I read your piece, I was reminded of Anne Frank who had to hide away in an attic in order to escape the Nazis. I wonder how Number the Stars is a story of survival.

I'm reading this year's Newbery award winner called Out of the Dust. Actually, it's the second time I have read the book. The writing is amazing. Each part of the story is like a poem. It's a different kind of survival story. It's like the picture book, The Dust Bowl, except it takes place in the United States. The families were victims of violent dust storms that ruined their crops. This girl is determined to get "out of the dust." (The author writes those four words more than twenty times throughout the book.)

Mr. Swartz

49: Responding Through Visuals

Some children may experience difficulty when writing prose to describe a book or summarize their reading. These children may benefit from presenting their material through the use of a graphic organizer or through art.

Graphic Organizers

There are four main types of graphic organizers that we can encourage young children to use to increase their comprehension: semantic maps, plot organizers, Venn diagrams and visual responses.

1. Semantic Maps

These maps can be used during prereading to record children's thoughts about what may be in the text, emerging from a brainstorming or discussion session. The activity focuses on activating prior knowledge and connecting to personal experiences. When illustrated through a semantic map, their experiences are acknowledged, respected, and grounded. They act as a firm base on which new concepts, revealed through the reading, are understood. One way to build a semantic map is to write the central word that represents the main idea of the text in the centre of a piece of paper, then write related categories in squares that are attached to the main word. Children then brainstorm details related to the categories. Semantic maps stimulate interest and confidence in reading, build vocabulary, and can serve as a teaching guide. They have been found to be particularly helpful for at-risk readers who have trouble recalling what they have read.

2. Plot Organizers

Plot organizers, an example of a post-reading activity, provide a visual means for organizing and analyzing plots and can often be geared directly to specific types of texts. These organizers help children summarize a plot and understand its organization, and they act as models for children writing their own stories. Specific plot organizers directly complement, represent, and heighten particular recurring plot patterns (e.g., circular, cumulative, count down) found in children's books. Plot-profile line graphs and cut-and-paste grids are examples of organizers where children rate events on books using horizontal and vertical axes (events are horizontal, ratings are vertical). Children's illustrations often accompany these organizers.

3. Venn Diagrams

A Venn diagram is an effective and concise graphic tool employed in post-reading contexts. It can represent comparisons and contrasting information within one story or book (e.g., settings) or between two or more books. A Venn diagram consists of two or more overlapping circles: the parts of the circles that do not intersect represent unique or contrasting attributes while the intersected sections depict shared or common characteristics that can be compared.

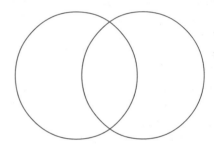

4. Art

Responding to a book through art frees children from worrying about their language abilities, a concern that many at-risk readers and ESL children share. A simple drawing of a poignant moment in the story speaks volumes about the child's reaction to a text.

There are many ways children can respond to text through art, including:
- creating a story quilt,
- constructing a visual time line,
- drawing a story map,
- illustrating what they believe is the most powerful moment in a story,
- capturing the mood of a text passage by making a simple sketch,
- creating masks for dramatizations,
- acting as an illustrator of a friend's story,
- writing a personal picture book patterned after or suggested by the story.

50: Reading Within a Theme

The act of reading does not stop at the end of the language arts period. Children employ their reading skills in all areas, from reading a math problem to reading reports on a topic related to social studies. Language skills of reading and writing form the basis for all of children's learning. To help them understand this interrelationship, we can develop themes that touch on aspects of several curriculum areas and illustrate the importance of reading and writing throughout the curriculum.

Developing a Thematic Unit

Themes can help children to see that what we learn in one area can help us in another. In this way, they come to understand and appreciate interrelationships both in and out of the classroom. Take, for example, the theme of birds at the primary level. Children can research the bird's history in North America – is it a native bird or was it "imported" (social studies), its height, weight and wingspan (math), and how it survives (science). They can draw a scaled replica of the bird (math), find references to the bird in works of literature (language arts), draw the bird in its habitat (art), create a rap about it (music), and write fact charts about the bird (language arts, science). Learning then, becomes less random as there is a natural progression and connection among subject areas.

Thematic units are most successful when exploring topics of interest to children. (Other, less appealing topics can be curtailed if children's interest is not sustained.) The value of themes can be extended through the use of a range of texts, including CD-ROMs, non-fiction books, magazines, newspapers, short stories, novels, and poetry books. Children participate in a range of activities through the day, exploring the topic from a variety of perspectives. The use of a range of texts can accommodate a wide range of reading abilities and interests, and the variety of texts helps children to utilize pragmatic cues (e.g., subheadings, margin notes, pictures). The boundaries of theme units are fluid as children react to new questions and issues that arise out of their research, and take responsibility for their learning.

Creating a Literacy Environment

One of the most important things we can do for children is to immerse them in an environment rich in quality texts of all genres. Given that children learn to read by reading, we want to ensure that the quality of texts they read is superior. We can read with children, to children, listen to them read aloud to us and to others, and observe them as they read independently and as part of a group. Children have the opportunity to hear words, see them, read them, and play with them.

Through this, stories and texts take children to new worlds and extend the boundaries of old worlds. We need to help children understand that what they know today can help them learn tomorrow, and that much of what we learn shares a connection with what we know. For this reason, we need to ensure that we include in class and school libraries books that reflect the cultures and issues represented and faced by the children in the classroom. They need to see themselves reflected in literature; they need to talk about real issues; and they need to see themselves as readers and writers, thinkers and learners who have something to contribute to the classroom and to the world at large.

Advantages of Thematic Learning

1. Connections between subjects, topics, and themes can be developed naturally to extend learning opportunities across the curriculum and throughout the day.
2. Learning is continuous and natural and moves beyond textbooks, curriculum guidelines, and time constraints.
3. Thematic units emphasize collaboration, cooperation, and process – not product.
4. Children's literature becomes an integral part of the curriculum.
5. The focus of children's work should be on individual problem solving, creative thinking, and critical thinking.
6. The concept of a "community of learners" is fostered.
7. Units allow for relevant, accurate assessment.
8. Through self-initiated learning activities and experiences, children have realistic, first-hand opportunities to initiate risk taking.
9. Children become active learners as they investigate connections between ideas and concepts, and reflect on their inquiries.

Steps to Developing and Implementing Thematic Units

1. Selecting the Theme
At this point, we need to consider the children's interests, the curriculum, relevant issues, and related events outside the school (e.g. field trips, community events). The theme should be broad enough to allow for a range of research and response, but not so broad that children will have difficulty linking concepts that are related to the theme.

2. Learning Outcomes and Curricular Area
We can list the attitudes, skills, and knowledge that children will gain and develop through participating in the unit, and the areas that they will work in (e.g., language arts, social studies, science, math, art, music, drama). We can decide on the most effective learning environment for the children (e.g., small groups, whole-class discussion, independent learning).

3. Resource Availability
The teacher will need to be familiar with resources (print, visual, human) that relate to the unit. Information sources include parents, people in the community, libraries, and resource centres.

4. Organizing the Theme
List and plan activities through a web. Children can add related ideas to be explored that spring from their work.

5. Brainstorming with the Class
We can introduce the theme and share unit plans, discussing with the children our level of knowledge, our interests, our attitudes, and our responses to the theme.

6. Selecting Resources
We can tailor the focus of the unit, based on the children's response to the brainstorming session.

7. Organizing the Classroom
The classroom will need to be organized to accommodate the unit – its activities, centres, and resources. We can use aids such as bulletin boards to support theme teaching by posting related materials that stimulate and motivate the children.

8. Implementing the Thematic Unit
The length of the unit will depend on its scope, the level of interest it creates, availability of resources, and your comfort level. Daily or weekly schedules of activities and outcomes can be posted that reflect your style and personal experience, and the needs of your students. Themes can range from a several days to several weeks (intermittent exploration).

9. Monitoring the Thematic Unit
Sharing projects and activities helps children to construct meaning, build a sense of community, and take ownership for their learning. By circulating and monitoring children's work, we can facilitate problem-solving, exploration, discovery, and investigative skills. Children can be encouraged to discuss their findings, pose and answer questions about their learning, and reflect on skills. As well, we can help children to make a connection between background and new knowledge, and reflect on their progress in relation to theme goals.

10. Evaluating and Reflecting
Discussions with children provide feedback for the unit. Was there sufficient time given? Was the topic too broad? Too narrow? How did it help the children grow? Feedback can be reflected on and incorporated when planning another unit study.

51: A Genre Study

Each genre of writing follows rules governing its format, the language patterns used, and its intended effect on a reader. Building a genre study is similar to studying a theme or engaging in an author study. However, instead of focusing on only one concept or on a limited selection of books from one author, children explore a type of writing, understanding the effect of the medium on the message.

Genre reading can be a helpful tool for children to explore, compare, describe, and assess types of books and various forms of writing. Knowing the characteristics of a genre can help children to model it in their writing.

Getting Started

One way to begin is to brainstorm with the children types of books they have read. With the children's input, one genre can be selected for study. Another way to begin is by choosing a genre that complements a theme children are looking at or represents a style of writing children want to explore. The choice of a genre may arise from observations of the children's choices of books from the library. We can choose a few books from this genre and read them aloud to the class, or discuss with the children titles from a genre that all have read. Together, we can generate a list of similar characteristics or patterns that are found in these books. This list and the follow-up activities will motivate children to think, read critically, and become more aware of their reading and writing.

We can set up a class library with books in the genre. Children can be encouraged to select related books from this library and to bring in books of their own. We can discuss with the children characteristics or rules of the genre and compare them with characteristics of another genre, charting similarities and differences.

Advantages of Genre Study

1. A genre study can be used as an organizational frame.
2. Genre study allows us to explore many topics, themes, and authors.
3. Genre study incorporates a large selection of books to work with, and is therefore able to accommodate the interests, preferences, capabilities, and needs of all children in the class.
4. Children are stimulated to read other books in the same genre or by the same author.
5. Children gain appropriate language to describe, compare, and talk about books, and are more comfortable sharing their reading experiences with peers.
6. Children will be able to relate books to other books (and to other genres).
7. Understanding print structures not only helps children understand what they read, but it also helps them to organize and to think about their writing.
8. Genre study provides a meaningful context for reading and writing.

Ideas for General Genre Study

1. Mapping
Have the children make a map that shows the location of adventures depicted in a novel.

2. Improvisation
Children form small groups to explore a genre. Group members can brainstorm characteristics of their genre before creating an oral story. They retell their story several times before making a tape.

3. True or False
Is the story real? Did the characters exist? Encourage the children to explore and research the places and events that are documented in a story (e.g., historical fiction, biography).

4. Time Line
Children can create time lines to plot technological breakthroughs and historical events detailed in science fiction, biography, or historical fiction books.

5. Fantasy World
After exploring fantasy or science fiction genres, children can create a world they read about. They can attach explanatory notes on their drawing, regarding inhabitants' appearance, culture, and value system. Children display their work.

6. The Future
Following a science fiction genre, ask the children to predict the future in the next fifty years. Ask them to describe advances in technology, medicine, and education, and ask them to list the technological aids that will make these advances possible.

7. Biography and Autobiography
At the end of a biography or autobiography genre study, children can choose someone they know that they would like to write about (they ask person's permission before beginning). Children conduct interviews with their subject and talk to others who know him or her. They use the results of their discussions in a biographical note that they share with the class.

52: An Author Unit

An author unit involves examination of a number of books written by the same author or author/illustrator. Children read the author's work, then discuss and write about it, and learn more about the author's life and motivation for writing. Children are often curious about authors many in the class have read. In this instance, they will have a working familiarity of the author and may want to read other works by him or her. We can gather these and other books, audiotape and videotape references to the author and his or her work, newspaper and magazine clippings, and dramatized forms of the author's work, if possible.

With the children's help, we can make a display of the author's work and life in the classroom. Children can read this material on their own, as part of a small group, or with our help.

Learning About an Author

1. Discussing the Author's Work
Discuss with the children patterns in the author's work, as well as common themes and the influence of the author's culture on writing. Together, compare his or her work with that of a similar author who writes in the same genre.

2. Responding Through Art
Children can respond to the author's work by creating a picture or collage that represents a moment in one of the author's works or the mood that overrides his or her books.

3. Responding Through Drama
Children form small groups of four or five members. They discuss favorite scenes of a book each member has read. Together, they choose and plan to present one of these scenes through mime, tableaux, or role-play. They practise their scene several times before presenting to other children. If audience members have also read the book, they try to guess the scene depicted.

4. Responding Through Writing
Children can write to the author care of his or her publisher, they can write about the author in their journal, or they can prepare a biography of their author, including a cover and backcover copy.

5. Picking a Favorite
When all the children in the class have read several of the author's books they can form groups based on their favorite book (if one book was clearly the favorite, divide the group into several smaller groups). Children can discuss their choice and list ways in which the title was superior to others written by the author.

6. Making a Historic Time Line
Children can create a decorative, historic time line that details important dates in an author's life (e.g, date and place of birth, schooling, dates when books were published).

7. Inviting an Author to Visit
Local authors or authors visiting the area can be invited to give a reading to a class or school. In advance of the visit, children can take part in an author study so they are prepared for the reading. As a follow-up to the author visit, children can write thank-you letters and share their responses to the reading.

Extension Ideas
1. Study more than one author at the same time, especially if the themes of their books can be linked.
2. Study authors who write in more than one genre (e.g., Eloise Greenfield).
3. Examine the relationship of an author to the illustrator. (Have they worked together before?)

53: A Non-Fiction Unit

In recent years, the quality of children's content books has risen dramatically, and many of these books can serve as an introduction to a vast array of topics. These books have the added advantage of helping you to assess children's present level of knowledge and give you the opportunity to model how to read such texts.

1. Introducing the Topic
As a large group, children can gather to listen as you read the text. As you read, note subtopics in the book. When you have finished reading, discuss the text as well as subtopics arising from the

reading. Children can choose one of the subtopics they wish to explore and form a group with other like-minded children, explore a topic independently, or work with a partner. Discuss the goals of the projects with each group of children, as well as ways in which their work will be assessed – self, peer, and teacher. In all instances, children note their questions as well as any knowledge they may have about the topic.

2. Researching the Topic
Children categorize their questions. When they have finished, they think about resources that will help them find the answers they need, including those in the class, in the school library, at home, and in the community. If working in a group, children take responsibility for one area of the project. For the next few days, they research their topic, tapping into sources of information they need.

3. Organizing the Information
When children have gathered all necessary information, they need to pool it and decide what form of presentation will best convey their information. (Some children will need help in choosing a form and may need to have you list options they can consider.) When children have made their choice, they gather materials they will need and prepare their work for publication/presentation.

4. Presenting the Learning
Each individual or group presents to the rest of the class. At the end of the presentation, children review the questions they had in the initial session. How many of their questions were answered? Which questions remain unanswered? They summarize knowledge they have learned and display their work so others may look at it over the next few weeks.

5. Assessing the Work
As the children work, note the behaviors of the children – their level of involvement, their use of strategies, their group skills. Review any self- and peer assessment matters with the children before they begin their presentations. As they present, assess the knowledge they have gained over the course of the unit as well as the quality of the publication/presentation. When determining overall assessments for the unit, include information from the self- and peer assessments.

Helping Children to Select Non-Fiction

When one considers that what we learn in history, in science, in geography, in art, is all story of one form or another, non-fiction begins to take on a new meaning. We need not consider these books something to wade through to research an idea. Many non-fiction books available today provide powerful experiences because they report on some of the most important historical, geographical, scientific, and artistic moments through time.

Children are fascinated by many aspects of the world around them – the power and fury of volcanoes, the preservation of forests thousands of years old, the unearthing of ancient civilizations, and the adventures of modern-day heroes. All good writing is literature, and many non-fiction writers are artists – they bring to life events and situations so that readers can share a part of that experience.

How we select non-fiction differs from how we approach a novel. We need to share this information with young children as they begin to sample the non-fiction genre.

To begin, non-fiction books contain a number of supports that we can check when selecting a title to read. With the children, you can model the following strategies:

1. Publication Date
Take a quick look at the publication date. If the topic you're exploring is a current issue, an older book may be helpful in providing background information, but you'll need to find other sources of information.

2. Table of Contents
Look at the book's table of contents since this tells readers what the book is about. Are the topics you're interested in covered in the table of contents?

3. Glossary
Some non-fiction books contain a glossary. Sample some of the words and their definitions. Are both difficult to understand? If yes, perhaps the book is intended for another audience.

4. Index
A quick review of an index can tell you exactly what the book contains and where to find information. It provides readers with a quick sense of the book's topic coverage.

5. Text

Sample a few paragraphs to determine the reading level. With the children, do a quick check of paragraphs through the book. Can you understand the main point of each paragraph? Is the vocabulary comprehensible? Is the text printed at a comfortable size for children?

6. Subheadings

A quick flip of a text indicates the presence of subheadings indicating the breakdown of material into chunks. Has the text been "chunked" so that children can read it with some degree of confidence?

7. Illustrations, Photographs, and Graphic Organizers

Many non-fiction texts support their information with visual components, such as illustrations, photographs, maps, charts, cross-sections, tables, and boxed text. As you skim the book, you can take a look at the visuals and sample some of them to determine their complexity.

How to Read Non-Fiction Books

Now that the selection has been made, you need to work with children to learn how to maximize time and effort when reading non-fiction.

1. Before You Read

Together, decide what it is you want to discover by reading the text. Make a list of the points they want to cover.

2. Pool Background Knowledge

What do you and the children know about the topic? Make short notes of existing knowledge the group shares on the topic.

3. Determine Important Knowledge

Not all information provided in a book will be useful. Look for chapter headings and subheadings that deal with information pertinent to your topic of study. Children can make notes of relevant information.

4. Watch for Important Words and Boxed Material

Words and phrases like "they found," "finally," and "in conclusion" usually signify important statements. Watch for boxed information that may summarize important points in a section.

5. Check Comprehension

Use visual supports to check what you have read and noted. Do they support your reading, or present new information? If it is a case of the latter, review what you have read. Have you misinterpreted information or missed reading important information?

6. Scan Material

Model skimming and scanning by reading aloud the material. Discuss with children how skimming and scanning can help you to read a piece quickly and reasons why you may want to do this (e.g., check for missing information, check for conflicting information, confirm information).

7. Review Learning

Review material gleaned from the book, then look at the questions you listed initially. How many questions were answered? Which questions remain unanswered? Did the book turn out to be a good source of information? If possible, children can divide the remaining questions and research them in other non-fiction books, following this model.

8. Record Bibliographic Information

Record the bibliographic information of each book used. Model the style of citing publications approved by your district.

Possible Topics of Research
- a topic related to curriculum
- a topic the child wants to explore
- an author
- an illustrator
- a topic related to a school event
- a topic related to a social event

Possible Sources of Information
- books
- CD-ROMs
- software
- nature walks
- observation
- museums
- magazines, newspapers
- the Internet
- audiotapes, videotapes
- guest speakers
- people in the community
- original source documents

54: Involving Parents in the Reading Process

The importance of time devoted to reading cannot be overlooked. In some homes, children will have been reading with their parents from the time they were toddlers. In other homes, reading may be considered a luxury that cannot be afforded.

We need to work with all parents to help them appreciate the crucial role reading can play in their child's development now and in the future. Parents also need to see the role they can play in their child's education, and that their voice is a valued addition and influence on learning.

One way to combine these factors is to institute a home reading program where children read independently for a set period each night (e.g., fifteen minutes for primary children, thirty minutes for junior children). Introduce the concept to the parents via a letter or a parent-child night. Parents can help their child read by reminding him or her of the time and providing a space away from the traffic of the house. Each child can be given a notebook, which they use as a reading log. When they begin the book, they note the title of the book, its author and illustrator (if applicable), and its genre. Each night after they finish reading, they can record the number of pages they read and write a brief response to the material read. Encourage the parents to discuss with the child his or her reading, and act as an audience should the child wish to read the material aloud.

Set aside ten minutes in the day when children can talk about their home reading with a peer who need not have read the same book.

It can be difficult to convince some parents that their support can help their child learn. We need to foster this attitude if we are to help all children become readers.

In addition to home reading programs, we can also involve parents in their child's education by asking them to serve as parent volunteers on a regular basis or on a special needs basis. Many parents need encouragement to enter a classroom, but once there can help in a number of ways, including listening to children read, scribing stories, going to the library to help with research, and sharing special knowledge.

A Guideline for Parents

1. Explore with your child how a book works – left to right, returning to left to start the next line (young readers).
2. Explore book information – a book's cover, pictures, text, back cover copy.
3. Note the child's responses to hearing a story read aloud, to shared reading, to reading aloud to you.
4. Remember that your child should read the story silently before reading sections aloud. You may want to read the book aloud to your beginning reader so that she or he can approach the book with some security.
5. If your child gets stuck, help him or her by asking, "What word would make sense here?" In some instances, you can help him or her by saying the sound of the first letter in a challenging word.
6. Check how your child determines the meaning of a word she or he does not know – looking at pictures, rereading the sentence, sounding out the word.
7. When a difficult word arises ask your child what word might work in this spot. Use the context of the story to make a connection, give a word that rhymes with the word, notice a small word or a group of letters within the word, omit the word and return to it later, or tell the child the word if it is important to the understanding of the text.
8. Help your child read a book on a new topic by talking about it and sharing some of what you know with your child. This gives your child some knowledge to help when reading.
9. Visit the library together. Note the books your child selects. Do they reflect his or her reading ability?
10. Talk about what your child likes to read and what she or he particularly likes or dislikes in a book.
11. Talk about your own reading, including your likes and dislikes. It is important for children to see models of reading at home. If you value reading, your child will likely value reading.
12. If your child uses a finger to read, don't worry. This helps the youngster to read, and the child will continue the practise only as long as necessary.
13. If your child wants to read a story again and again, read it. Many children have favorites and enjoy the familiarity the text brings. The reading is not without value because the child reinforces the learning.

14. Don't worry about correcting every mistake your child makes while reading aloud, particularly those mistakes where the meaning isn't changed. If your child does make a lot of meaning mistakes, discuss the topic before continuing the reading.

15. If your child has tried to read a book, but is not interested in it, don't force the child to read it. We all start books that we never finish. Use the baseball analogy: "Three tries and then I choose."

16. Note your child's changing tastes in books and the amount of time your child can read without losing attention.

17. Literacy doesn't begin and end with books. Encourage your child to listen to book tapes and watch films of books.

18. As your child reads aloud, notice how the reading sounds. Is it choppy, or is it smooth? If it is choppy, the child may be reading a book that is too challenging. Ask your child, "Would like me to read aloud with you?"

19. Talk to me about your observations and experiences. The information you have is very important to your child's reading program. If we work together, we can develop a reading program that best meets your child's needs and interests.

All parents need to know what is happening in their child's classroom. You can share this knowledge by creating a home-school journal that you can send home with the child. You can make notes of the child's reading program at school, as well as other news; the parent can record his or her observations of the child's reading experiences at home.

55: Using Information Technologies to Promote Literacy

Computer educator Rikie Schieven has created the following suggestions for incorporating information technology into our classrooms and into new literacy programs. (See pages 103–107)

Why do we talk to our children before they understand? Why do we allow them to take a few halting steps knowing they'll fall – and try again?

Why do we, as teachers, have sandboxes in our classrooms ? The answer to all of these questions is that each activity is a building block for so many that come later. Without a myriad of early experiences, the tasks of learning to make meaning of language, of learning to read, and of learning to write would be a much more difficult process. Each element must be mastered before more difficult and complex tasks may be tried.

In the same way, young children need to build skills in using computers. Many children who treat the computer as they did a sandbox, learn not to fear technology but to make it their friend. As they compose their stories and reports, children acquire skills in using a mouse, locating letters on a keyboard, typing text, and using simple graphics tools. These children are mastering basic components of the computer and are preparing for the higher end activities that will come in subsequent grades.

There are those who will cry out that computers are antisocial, and take away from the concrete activities in which children must engage. No one ever suggested that the physical and social aspects in the early grades should be removed to make way for computers. All activities must be balanced; each is part of a whole. Children must have access to activities that will help them become good learners, as well as be physically and socially healthy. Anyone who has watched the excitement and sharing that takes place around a computer will know that social skills are enhanced with this tool. Much research has been done to show that children, positive learning, and computers go well together.

Research supporting the use of computers in the classroom has been overwhelmingly supportive – many children seem to find using the computer a liberating approach to writing, and they develop a more positive approach to learning. More current research shows even more positive aspects of computer use. The development of a sense of purpose, understanding the connections between their work and the real world, a willingness to rework ideas and drafts, sharing with peers, using higher level thinking skills, and developing more complex problem-solving abilities were all areas of growth for the children in these schools.

In addition to research examples, there are also numerous anecdotes in the literature from teachers who describe how children changed as a result of excellent use of computers. One story involves three children in a self-contained class for children with learning disabilities. These children had major problems getting anything on paper, more often than not ending a writing session by furiously crumpling their pages into balls and flinging them away in total frustration. The addition of computers into the program allowed them to work on their ideas rather than the physical process of writing. First came halting sentences, then short paragraphs. Within six months, these junior level children were writing chapter books! The most interesting part of the story occurred after they had been in the program for a year and a half. One day, one of the children asked if she could write her story by hand! Her self-confidence had increased to such a high degree that she was now able to choose handwriting as an option.

Teachers have frequently commented on the enthusiasm with which children embrace technology. We must not allow our fears and hesitations to prevent children from having access to this powerful tool. Information technologies free children from physical constraints, motivate them, allow them to connect with others around the world, provide them with purpose for their projects, and give them access to powerful problem-solving tools. From the simplest talking CD-ROM that allows a non-reader to enjoy a story to the hypermedia software that gives children the power to create their own multimedia presentations to Internet projects that connect us to others around the world, computers are a tool that will empower children as nothing else can.

Benefits of Using Computers in the Literacy Program

1. The quality and fluency of writing is increased. Children provide more details and revise more. As well, they confer with us more frequently, thus becoming more involved in the writing process.
2. The amount of talk about text is increased, as well as error detection in peers' writing.
3. The concept of publishing motivates children to write and read.
4. Some programs are specifically designed to help children develop planning processes in writing, narrative writing skills, expressive writing, and revision and editing skills.
5. Computers can be used for a variety of writing activities, including letters, stories, poems, messages, mail, newspapers, banners, book logs, and journals.
6. CD-ROMs can provide children with an abundance of information that could once be housed only in encyclopedias and large reference materials.
7. Along with a modem, computers can provide an authentic and interactive means for children to write to one another. Some classrooms have begun sharing journals with classes in other towns and cities, and even in other countries.
8. The Internet allows children to research any number of topics and receive current information. It removes barriers once faced by children in rural areas as they can access the same information as their urban counterparts.

Considerations for Using the Internet

Most of us are aware of the great advantages the Internet offers children. We are also aware of potential drawbacks, including:

- a lack control over quality. The adage "buyer beware" can be borrowed here to become "reader beware." Anyone can post a web site on the Internet, and as a result, information is not checked for accuracy. Encourage children to use web sites from established institutions and businesses.
- a lack of control over harmful sites. As stated, anyone can post a web site. We need to observe children as they use the Internet to ensure that they are where they should be.
- varying search engines. Not all search engines are created equal. As well, some children will be able to manoeuvre in any environment, while others will search in vain for hours. Proficient peers can act as tutors to classmates who have less experience finding information on the Internet.
- time. We need to limit children's time on the Internet given the demand for use by other children. Wandering the Internet, while entertaining, can be extremely time consuming.

56: Information Sources In and Out of the School

Classroom Resources

In the classroom, we have several potential sources of information. One, of course, is the class book collection. A second includes children, who may have a specialized knowledge of a particular topic because of an intense interest in it, or because of a family member's career or hobby. To be able to tap into these "human" resources, children need to share with others special bodies of knowledge. Children can advertise their special knowledge in a "Professional Knowledge Available" column in a class newspaper or post it on the class bulletin board. Children from other classrooms and school staff can be encouraged to add their listing so children have a wide range of school sources to draw on.

Library Resources

The library (and the librarian) are sources of information for all children in the school. The role of libraries is ultimately for the benefit and development of the child and therefore must provide and utilize the most effective human, material, and physical resources possible. So, in addition to the print resources a library offers, many libraries have computers equipped with a CD-ROM and Internet access. With some help from the librarian, children can access these sources.

Classroom and School Visitors

In many areas, several programs, such as Artists-in-the-Schools, help schools to bring guest artists and authors to present demonstrations and readings to children. As well, the community can be a source of guest speakers, such as artists, musicians, athletes, people associated with organizations, business people, parents who have interesting careers, retired people, and health professionals. In addition, we can be aware of events such as cultural events and historical displays that children can benefit from visiting.

An A to Z of Information Sources

Advertisements... Books, books, and more books... Children's shows and videos... Dramas... Educational software... Folklore... Games... Historical documents... Interviews... Journals... Knowledge – from other children, people in the community... Letters... Modems to access the Internet... Networking... Opera... Pictures... Quotations... Reference materials... Spreadsheets...Television...United Nations and other organizations... Videos... Writings of others... Xerox and other large businesses... Year-end reports... Zoos, museums, and other public institutions

57: Assessing and Evaluating Young Readers

When we discuss assessment, we talk about the ongoing observation of children, including anecdotal observations, conferences, reading profiles and checklists, and portfolios. Outcomes of assessment procedures allow us to plan programs for children that reflect their current learning and capitalize on their strengths to develop other areas of growth. Evaluation refers to the judgements we make on the basis of our assessment practices. Assessment, then, informs our daily teaching, and evaluation – marks and grades – is used when communicating with parents and other educators.

The quality of our evaluation reflects our assessment procedures. We need to assess all areas of a child's development and, in order to do this, we need to gather information, in addition to the methods listed above, from others in the school and from the child's parents. We need to look at the books the child reads, the amount read, the degree of pleasure derived from reading, the strategies used, the quality of the responses, the ability to reflect on the learning, the awareness of the elements of the reading process, and the ability to self-assess personal reading growth.

You can share with the children your goals of assessment and the role they play in shaping their reading program. Like you, the children need to track their learning, (including books they have read, reflections on reading, response methods they have used, areas in which they are confident and skills they would like to improve), collect pieces they have published, and organize peer and self-assessments.

The checklists in this book support your documentation of each child's progress in reading. Analyzing and collating the information from these checklists will provide you with the information you need to

- plan effective reading programs,
- group and regroup children according to their abilities, needs, and interests,
- report to parents, and
- provide end-of-year assessments.

Your assessment tools, combined with those completed by the children, can provide you with a well-rounded analysis of each child's abilities.

58: Observing Young Readers

While we are observing children, we bring to the process our knowledge of the theory of language learning and the practical aspects of teaching the children to read. There are two main types of observation: close observation and distance observation. Close observation involves observing a child for a period of five minutes while she or he reads. You can note the book the child reads, the strategies she or he uses, aspects of the text that appear to be challenging, and what the child does when she or he encounters difficulty. Distance observation involves watching the child for a similar amount of time as she or he selects a book, the amount of time the child can read independently, and the amount of movement the child exhibits during the activity. In order to observe the children to a sufficient degree, we need to make observations of one or two children each day, or devote one day a week to observation.

When possible, tape children's discussions and presentations. Viewing the tapes, away from the bustle of the classroom, provides you with information relating to children's participation in groups, the level of discussions in which children engage, and individual strengths and weaknesses. Additionally, tapes allow you to assess your level and type of involvement in the groups.

Observation Guides and Checklists

It is important to remember that, as useful as they are, observation guides and checklists are just that – indicators of a child's progress. On their own,

no one guide can be viewed as absolute: its value lies in the information it can contribute to the overall analysis of a child's reading growth.

Checklists and guides are most valuable when they are repeated several times through the year. In this way, trends and progress that occur over the year can be noted. They help to tell us how a child is developing as a reader – the level of fluency, use of strategies and awareness of cueing systems. Observations arising from the checklists can be shared with the children in order to help them focus on areas that require change.

The following modes of assessment can add to an understanding of a child's progress as a successful reader:

- responses to open-ended questions
- literature response journals
- writing journals
- self-evaluations
- completed enterprises / projects / activities / assignments / reports / research / graphs / charts / illustrations
- child-initiated questions / tests
- notebooks
- writing folders
- reading records of books read
- word banks
- writing samples (plays, poems, letters, stories, published pieces)
- responses through visual arts portfolios
- teacher-made tests
- standardized achievement tests
- minimum competency tests
- school, district, or provincial tests
- norm-referenced tests
- writing vocabulary
- spelling tests, vocabulary tests
- diagnostic tests/surveys
- observation guides and checklists

59: Portfolio Assessment

Portfolio conferences about reading are an invaluable source of information about a child's reading experiences. Children bring to the conference several journal entries to discuss with you their growth as readers. Informal discussion questions may relate to the number of books read, the number of books begun but not finished, and the reasons. Based on the results of the conference, you can conduct reading inventories and/or set new goals (e.g., setting a number of pages, books to be read; reading books from another genre), and work together to assess reading progress.

Portfolio conferences can take place between you and the child, between peers, or between a parent and a child. Of these configurations, teacher-child conferences are essential, peer conferences are desirable (depending on the age of the children), and child-parent conferences are recommended. Your conferences with children are essential for the development of self-assessment skills. Only when you have had a conference with each child should the children participate in peer conferences. Ongoing child-teacher conferences may culminate in child-led parent conferences at the end of the year.

Parents must be prepared to participate in, and respond meaningfully to, their child's presentation. To facilitate this, you can send home a letter with guidelines or discuss the process with parents in advance (e.g., at the previous reporting interview). During the child-led parent conference, you act as a resource person, giving input only when requested. Twenty minutes to a half-hour is recommended for each conference, and you can participate in four conferences at a time simultaneously.

A Portfolio Synopsis

- Read and review professional literature that relates to portfolios.
- Review your goals for creating and using portfolios. How will you use them to plan programs? How will you share them with learners? How will you report the results of the portfolios with children's parents and caregivers?
- Create a portfolio for yourself. Share it with the children.
- Discuss with the children and collect materials that you can use to make a portfolio (e.g., a scrapbook, a box, a file folder). Encourage children to be creative when they decorate their portfolios.
- Outline the purposes of the portfolio.
- Hold a large-class discussion of what the portfolios should include. Discuss with them the frequency with which items will be included in the portfolio. Draw their attention to the fact that pieces in the portfolio can originate outside of the classroom.
- Discuss with children forms to be included in the portfolio, including a reading log form, a conference reflection form, a self-assessment form, and a peer evaluation form.
- Ask children to consider who will view the contents of the portfolio.
- Give mini-lessons and demonstrations on maintaining a portfolio.
- Share with the children pieces from portfolios in past years (block out the child's name). Illustrate aspects of the piece and ask children to comment on the pieces.
- Ensure that children have time to assess pieces they wish to include on their portfolio as well as the necessary time to polish these pieces. As their use evolves, identify areas where children may benefit from a mini-lesson.
- Discuss with children which pieces they can take home and which pieces will remain in the portfolio.
- Illustrate to the children how you will assess portfolio pieces.
- Use the portfolios in student-teacher conferences and parent-teacher-child conferences.
- Monitor the portfolios on a regular basis.

Possible Contents of the Portfolio

- a table of contents (to organize their entries)
- an "About the Author" piece (preliminary piece)
- drawings, pictures, photos, and/or descriptions of favorite people, places and things
- letters (e.g., to authors, characters in books, heroes in myths and fables)
- reading responses (e.g., assigned work, journal entries, notes made in and out of the classroom)
- drafts and final versions of writing (assigned and free writing)
- selected journal entries
- notes on ideas, observations, experiences, and interests
- audiotapes and videotapes, computer disks
- captions included on each piece that describe why the child chose to include it
- reading and writing logs, which include for each book its title, author, date, and a brief response
- memorable quotes
- pieces written by others the child admires
- a reading list for the coming months

- a list of books rated by difficulty, genre, and response
- indepth book reviews
- a synopsis of a group's discussion of a book
- interesting words children have met in their reading and in conversation
- words they have met this year and mastered
- comments from you, the child's parents, his or her peers
- selections that the child wants to share from school, home, or elsewhere that show him or her as a reader, writer, speaker, listener, actor, poet, person!
- a child's résumé that documents learning to date
- comparisons of authors, genres, and books within a series
- samples of e-mail printouts
- drafts of a published piece
- child's contributions to class writing, such as newspapers and displays
- letters, including letters to the editor, letters you have written to the child, and letters the child has written to you
- questionnaires the child has contributed to
- writing-in-role selections
- miscue analyses
- running record samples

60: Anecdotal Records

Inventories, where children complete a list of their achievements, favorite activities, and interests, can be extremely helpful when planning topics to explore in class. In addition, inventories can tell you about a child's feelings related to aspects of their learning and information that may not be visible in class. Ideally, children can complete inventories with their parents when they begin school in September. In-class inventories related to materials read can be updated throughout the year.

Anecdotal records are those we make on an informal basis as we observe children in their day-to-day learning. Given the nature of these observations, many teachers choose to make notes on index cards or a small notepad. In this instance, you can write the child's name at the bottom of the card, which can be stored in an open file. You can observe children by groups or on an individual basis. Another method involves the use of

a file folder divided into 3x3 squares. Write children's names in the squares and observations of their behavior (dated) on similar-sized sticky notes that you place on the square. At the end of each week, you can transfer the notes to a letter-sized piece of paper, which can then be stored in the child's folder.

61: Formal and Informal Tests

Tests, formal and informal, are helpful when they assess learning that is measurable and when they reflect the content of the program. However, in reading many components cannot be isolated. For this reading, interpretation of reading tests must be handled carefully. If information gleaned from the tests does not reflect your ongoing assessment, the testing device may need to be altered. A less likely scenario involves adjusting your ongoing assessment.

If both the test and the instruction are sound, there are a number of reasons a child may not perform well on an isolated test, ranging from a bad night's rest to a problem at home – the test results should be viewed by both you and the students as a way to check the effectiveness of the program. In this way, children will feel less anxious and not be concerned that a poor test result will influence their learning for the rest of the year.

In some areas of the country, class-wide testing is becoming more common. Much has been made, in some areas, of lower than expected results and a call for action has resulted. What we need to keep in mind is that, just as in individual cases, a variety of factors may influence reading results. One evident example is a class where the majority of the class speak English as a second language. These factors must be taken into account when discussing such results. We also need to consider the fact that in such situations one test for all may not be the most effective measure.

62: Reporting to Parents

As we all know, reporting on a child's reading ability differs somewhat from reporting on his or her math skills. Many of the strategies and skills needed to become a fluent reader do not lend themselves to a numerical score. We need to share this with parents, and reassure them that there are other, less obvious ways of measuring growth, including charting books read, conducting running records with the child, conferring with him or her on a regular basis, monitoring progress through the use of checklists, and assessing the depth to which a child understands what she or he reads through written responses.

The reintroduction of standardized testing has also led many parents to compare their child's performance to others in the class, in another school, and in other districts. We need to reassure them that what is important is how their child has developed through the school year. We can show them this by providing responses their child has written during the year.

We know the importance of involving a child in the outline of his or her program. Parents, too, can play an important role in the education of their child. When we outline the goals of our program, share with them the techniques we use to reach these goals, and outline the tools and methods we use to assess their child, parents have a more complete picture of their child's education. They can contribute to the process by observing their child's reading behavior at home and discussing their findings in three-way conferences between parent, child, and teacher, a necessary part of any child's assessment.

63: Self-Assessment – Child and Teacher

Self-assessment is a critical element of a child's reading program. When children know that self-assessment will form a part of their overall assessment, they develop a sense of ownership of their learning and know that they can shape the course of their learning. They are active participants who help to shape the reading program. Their contributions in conferences, journals, portfolios, and discussions with you and their peers are all part of the self-assessment process. Sharing in their assessment helps children to recognize what they know, what they need to know, and ways in which they can learn. Children begin to see themselves as readers and writers, thinkers and meaning makers.

There are a variety of ways children can assess their learning. They can complete checklists, review their portfolios and, through the use of taped audiotapes and videotapes, assess their contribution to group discussions and responses to texts.

In addition to assessing and evaluating children, we need to evaluate our teaching programs. When we self-evaluate, we check on the program's ability to meet the goals we set for children. In part, program evaluation arises from the progress children make. We can also complete questionnaires to help us reflect on our teaching practices. We need to ensure that what we do in class, from selecting texts through assessing a child's responses, are sound, valid, and contribute to children's overall development.

64: Checklists and Guidelines

Program Evaluation

In addition to assessing and evaluating children, we need to continually examine and modify our teaching programs. When we self-evaluate, we check on the program's ability to meet the goals we set for children. In part, program evaluation arises from the progress children make. We can also use the checklists, guidelines and rubrics in the appendix to help us reflect on our teaching practices. We need to ensure that what we do in class, from selecting texts through assessing a child's responses, are worthwhile and positive, and contribute to the children's overall development.

65: Reading with Prereaders

Ahlberg, Allan and Janet. *Each Peach Pear Plum.* New York, NY: Viking.

Ahlberg, Allan and Janet. *Peepo.* London, UK: Puffin.

Asch, Frank. *I Can Blink.* Toronto, ON: Kids Can. (Also: *I Can Roar.*)

Asch, Frank. *Just Like Daddy.* Englewood Cliffs, NJ: Prentice-Hall.

Baker, Keith. *Big Fat Hen.* San Diego, CA: Harcourt Brace.

Bang, Molly. *Ten, Nine, Eight.* New York, NY: Greenwillow.

Barton, Byron. *Dinosaurs, Dinosaurs.* New York, NY: Crowell.

Bourgeois, Paulette. *Franklin.* (Series). Illustrated by Brenda Clark. Toronto, ON: Kids Can.

Brown, Margaret Wise. *Goodnight Moon.* New York, NY: Harper and Row.

Bruna, Dick. *Miffy!* (Series). New York, NY: Kodansha.

Burningham, John. *Mr. Gumpy's Outing.* New York, NY: Puffin Books.

Burningham, John. *The Dog.* (Series). New York, NY: Crowell.

Carle, Eric. *The Grouchy Ladybug.* New York, NY: Philomel.

Cousins, Lucy. *Za-Za's Baby Brother.* Cambridge, MA: Candlewick.

Ehlert, Lois. *Eating the Alphabet.* San Diego, CA: Harcourt Brace.

Fleming, Denise. *Lunch.* New York, NY: Henry Holt.

Fox, Mem. *Time For Bed.* Illustrated by Jane Dyer. San Diego, CA: Harcourt Brace.

Hill, Eric. *Spot's First Walk.* (Series). New York, NY: Putnam.

Hoban, Tana. *Red, Blue, Yellow Shoe.* (Series). New York, NY: Greenwillow.

Hughes, Shirley. *Playing.* Boston, MA: Candlewick.

Hutchins, Pat. *Rosie's Walk.* New York, NY: Scholastic.

Kovalski, Maryann. *The Wheels on the Bus.* Toronto, ON: Kids Can. (Also: *Take Me Out to the Ballgame; Jingle Bells.*)

Kraus, Ruth. *The Carrot Seed.* Illustrated by Crockett Johnson. New York, NY: Scholastic.

Martin, Jr., Bill. *Brown Bear, Brown Bear, What Do You See?* Illustrated by Eric Carle. New York, NY: Henry Holt.

Martin, Jr., Bill and John Archambault. *Chicka Chicka Boom, Boom.* New York, NY: Simon and Schuster.

Martin, Jr., Bill. *Polar Bear, Polar Bear, What Do You Hear?* Illustrated by Eric Carle. New York, NY: Henry Holt.

Mayer, Mercer. *Oops.* New York, NY: Penguin.

McBratney, Sam and Anita Jeram. *Guess How Much I Love You.* London, UK: Walker.

Opie, Iona. *My Very First Mother Goose.* Illustrated by Rosemary Wells. New York, NY: Dial.

Pilkey, Dav. *Big Dog and Little Dog.* (Series). San Diego, CA: Harcourt Brace.

Rockwell, Anne. *Boats.* New York, NY: Penguin.

Rylant, Cynthia. *Everyday Children.* (Series). New York, NY: Bradbury Press.

Serfozo, Mary. *Who Said Red?* New York, NY: Simon and Schuster.

Simon, Francesca and Susan Winter. *Calling All Toddlers.* London, UK: Orion.

Stinson, Kathy. *Red Is Best.* Toronto, ON: Annick.

Tafuri, Nancy. *Have You Seen My Duckling?* New York, NY: Morrow.

Wells, Rosemary. *Max's First Word.* (Series). New York, NY: Dial.

Wildsmith, Brian. *Cat on the Mat.* London, UK: Oxford.

66: Books for Emerging Readers

Allinson, Beverley. *Effie.* Toronto, ON: Scholastic.

Bang, Molly. *Wiley and the Hairy Man.* New York, NY: Macmillan.

Bannerman, Helen. *The Story of Little Babaji.* Illustrated by Fred Marcellino. New York, NY: HarperCollins.

Bemelmans, Ludwig. *Madeline.* (Series). New York, NY: Viking.

Bogart, Jo Ellen. *Daniel's Dog.* Toronto, ON: Scholastic.

Bourgeois, Paulette. *Franklin.* (Series). Illustrated by Brenda Clarke. Toronto, ON: Kids Can.

Brett, Jan. *The Mitten*. New York, NY: Scholastic.

Brown, Marcia. *The Three Billy Goats*. New York, NY: Harcourt Brace.

Brown, Mark. *Arthur*. (Series). New York, NY: Little Brown.

Browne, Anthony. *Willy and Hugh*. (Series). Toronto, ON: Douglas and McIntyre.

Burningham, John. *Cloudland*. London, UK: Jonathan Cape.

Chase, Edith Newlin. *The New Baby Calf*. Richmond Hill, ON: Scholastic.

Cohen, Miriam. *Jim's Dog Muffins*. New York, NY: Dell.

Cohen, Miriam. *Lost in the Museum*. (Series). Illustrated by Lillian Hoban. New York, NY: Dell.

Ehlert, Lois. *Snowballs*. San Diego, CA: Harcourt Brace. (Also: *Growing Vegetable Soup; Eating the Alphabet; Red Leaf, Yellow Leaf; Hands*.)

Fox, Mem. *Wilfred Gordon McDonald Partridge*. New York, NY: Kane/Miller.

Gilman, Phoebe. *Jillian Jiggs*. (Series). Toronto, ON: Scholastic.

Gilman, Phoebe. *Something From Nothing*. Toronto, ON: Scholastic.

Ginsburg, Mirra. *Across the Stream*. Illustrated by Nancy Tafuri. New York, NY: Greenwillow.

Goodwin, Laura. *Little White Dog*. New York, NY: Hyperion.

Hoban, Lillian. *Arthur's Back to School Day*. (Series). New York, NY: Harper Trophy.

Hoban, Russell. *Bread and Jam for Frances*. New York, NY: Harper & Row.

Johnson, Crockett. *Harold and the Purple Crayon*. (Series). New York, NY: Harper & Row.

Jonas, Ann. *Round Trip*. New York, NY: Greenwillow. (Also: *The Trek; The 13th Clue; Reflections; Watch William Walk*.)

Joyce, William. *George Shrinks*. New York, NY: HarperCollins.

Keats, Ezra Jack. *The Snowy Day*. New York, NY: Collier.

Keats, Ezra Jack. *Whistle for Willie*. New York, NY: Penguin.

Kraus, Robert. *Leo The Late Bloomer*. Illustrated by José Aruego. (Sequel: Little Louie the Baby Bloomer.) New York, NY: Windmill.

Kraus, Robert. *Where Are You Going, Little Mouse?* New York, NY: Greenwillow.

Lobel, Arnold. *Days With Frog and Toad*. New York, NY: HarperCollins.

Marshall, Edward. *Fox and His Friends*. (Series). New York, NY: Dial.

Marshall, James. *George and Martha*. (Series). New York, NY: Houghton Mifflin.

Marshall, James. *The Three Little Pigs*. New York, NY: Scholastic.

Marzollo, Jean. *I Spy*. (Series). Photographs by Walter Wick. New York, NY: Scholastic.

Mayer, Mercer. *If I Had An Alligator*. New York, NY: Dial.

McCloskey, Robert. *Make Way For Ducklings*. New York, NY: Viking.

McPhail, David. *Edward and the Pirates*. Boston, MA: Little Brown.

Meadowbooks: Level A, Level B. Toronto, ON: Harcourt Brace

Meddaugh, Susan. *Five Little Piggies*. Boston, MA: Houghton Mifflin.

Minerik, Else Holmelund. *Little Bear's Visit*. (Series). Illustrated by Maurice Sendak. New York, NY: Harper & Row.

Morgan, Allen. *Sadie and the Snowman*. Toronto, ON: Scholastic.

Most, Bernard. *Pets in Trumpets*. San Diego, CA: Harcourt Brace.

Munsch, Robert. *Alligator Baby*. Toronto, ON: Scholastic.

Numeroff, Laura. *If You Give a Pig a Pancake*. Illustrated by Felicia Bond. New York, NY: Harper Collins.

Oppenheim, Joanne. *Have You Seen Birds?* Toronto, ON: Scholastic.

Raffi. *Everything Grows*. ("Song to Read" Series). New York, NY: Crown.

Raschka, Chris. *Yo! Yes?* New York, NY: Orchard.

Reid, Barbara. *The Party*. Toronto, ON: North Winds.

Rey, H.A. *Curious George*. (Series). Boston, MA: Houghton Mifflin.

Rosen, Michael. *We're Going on a Bear Hunt*. Illustrated by Helen Oxenbury. London, UK: Walker.

Sendak, Maurice. *Where The Wild Things Are*. New York, NY: HarperCollins.

Seuss, Dr. *One Fish Two Fish Red Fish Blue Fish*. New York, NY: Random House.

Shaw, Nancy. *Sheep in a Jeep*. New York, NY: Scott Foresman.

Steig, William. *Doctor De Soto*. Farrar, Straus and Giroux.

Taylor, Judy. *My Dog*. New York, NY: Macmillan.

Titherington, Jeanne. *Pumpkin, Pumpkin*. New York, NY: Greenwillow.

Van Leeuwen, Jean. *Tales of Oliver Pig*. (Series). Illustrated by Arnold Lobel. New York, NY: Dial.

Wadell, Martin. *Farmer Duck*. London, UK: Walker.

Watanabe, Shigeo. *How Do I Put It On?* (Series).

Wells, Rosemary. *Bunny Money*. (Max and Ruby Series). New York, NY: Dial.

Wells, Rosemary. *Noisy Nora*. New York, NY: Scholastic.

Yardley, Joanna. *The Red Ball*. San Diego, CA: Harcourt Brace.

Young, Ed. *Seven Blind Mice*. New York, NY: Philomel.

Zion, Gene. *Harry the Dirty Dog*. (Series). Illustrated by Margaret B. Graham. New York, NY: Harper & Row.

67: Books for Transitional Developing Readers

Allen, Judy. *Tiger*. Cambridge, MA: Candlewick. (Also: *Eagle, Elephant, Panda, Whale*.)

Betancourt, Jane. *Pony Pals*. (Series). New York, NY: Scholastic.

Blume, Judy. *Freckle Juice*. New York, NY: Dell Yearling.

Bourgeois, Paulett. *Grandma's Secret*. Toronto, ON: Kids Can.

Cannon, Janell. *Stellaluna*. San Diego, CA: Harcourt Brace. (Also: *Verdi*.)

Cherry, Lynne. *The Great Kapok Tree*. San Diego, CA: Harcourt Brace.

Cleary, Beverly. *Maggie Muggie*. New York, NY: Avon Camelot.

Cole, Joanna. *Magic School Bus*. (Series). New York, NY: Scholastic.

Fitch, Sheree. *There Were Monkeys in the Kitchen*. Illustrated by Marc Mongeau. Toronto, ON: Doubleday.

Greenfield, Eloise. *Nathaniel Talking*. Illustrated by Jan Spivey Gilchrest. New York, NY: Black Butterfly.

Heide, Florence Parry and Judith Heide Gilliland. *The Day of Ahmed's Secret*. New York, NY: Lothrop, Lee and Shepard.

Henkes, Kevin. *Chrysanthemum*. New York, NY: Greenwillow. (Also: *Lily's Purple Plastic Purse; Owen; Sheila Rae the Brave*.)

Lottridge, Celia. *The Name of the Tree*. Illustrated by Ian Wallace. Toronto, ON: Douglas and McIntyre.

McFarlane, Sheryl. *Waiting for the Whales*. Illustrated by Ron Lightburn. Victoria, BC: Orca.

Meadowbooks: Level C. Toronto, ON: Harcourt Brace

Parish, Peggy. *Amelia Bedelia*. (Series). New York, NY: Greenwillow.

Roy, Ron. *The Absent Author*. ("A to Z Mysteries" Series). New York, NY: Random House.

Ryder, Joanna. *Catching the Wind*. ("Just for a Day" Series). New York, NY: Morrow.

Rylant, Cynthia. *Henry and Midge*. (Series). New York, NY: Bradbury.

Rylant, Cynthia. *The Relatives Came*. New York, NY: Bradbury.

Sharmat, Marjorie Weinman. *Dog-gone Hollywood*. New York, NY: Random House.

Silverstein, Shel. *The Giving Tree*. New York, NY: HarperCollins.

Van Allsburg, Chris. *Jumanji*. Boston, MA: Houghton Mifflin.

Yashima, Taro. *Crow Boy*. New York, NY: Viking.

Ziefert, Harriet. *Small Potatoes Club*. (Series). New York, NY: Dell.

68: Books for Developing Readers

Adler, David A. *Cam Jansen*. (Series). New York, NY: Puffin.

Bauer, Marion Dane. *On My Honor*. New York, NY: Clarion.

Blume, Judy. *Tales of a Fourth Grade Nothing*. New York, NY: Dell.

Christopher, Matt. *Wingman on Ice*. (Sports Series). New York, NY: Little, Brown.

Cleary, Beverly. *The Mouse and the Motorcycle*. (Also: *Ralph S. Mouse; Runaway Ralph*.) New York, NY: Dell Yearling.

Dadey, Debbie and Marcia Thornton Jones. *The Adventures of The Bailey School Kids*. (Series). New York, NY: Scholastic.

Dahl, Roald. *James and the Giant Peach.* New York, NY: Alfred A. Knopf.

Danziger, Paula. *Amber Brown.* (Series). New York, NY: Scholastic.

Delton, Judy. *Pee Wee Scouts.* (Series). New York, NY: Dell Yearling.

Gardiner, John Reynolds. *Stone Fox.* New York, NY: HarperCollins.

Giff, Patricia Reilly. *Polk Street School.* (Series). New York, NY: Dell Yearling.

Howe, James and Deborah. *Bunnicula.* (Series). New York, NY: Camelot.

Hughes, Ted. *The Iron Man.* (Sequel: *The Iron Woman*). London, UK: Faber.

King-Smith, Dick. *The Sheep Pig.* London, UK: Puffin.

Kinsey-Warnock, Natalie. *The Canada Geese Quilt.* New York: Dutton.

LeGuin, Ursula K. *Catwings.* (Sequel: *Catwings Return.*) New York, NY: Scholastic.

Levy, Elizabeth and Mordicai Gerstein. *Something Queer at the Ball Park.* (Series). New York, NY: Dell.

Little, Jean. *Different Dragons.* Toronto, ON: Penguin.

MacLachlan. *Sarah, Plain and Tall.* (Sequel: *Skylark*). New York, NY: Harper Row.

Meadowbooks: Level 4. Toronto, ON: Harcourt Brace

Osborne, Mary Pope. *Magic Tree House.* (Series). New York, NY: Random House.

Park, Barbara. *Junie B. Jones.* (Series). New York, NY: Random House.

Park, Barbara. *Mick Harte Was Here.* New York, NY: Random House.

Pilkey, Dav. *The Adventures of Captain Underpants.* New York, NY: Scholastic.

Sachar, Louis. *Sideways Stories From a Wayside School.* (Series). New York, NY: Avon Camelot.

Scieszka, Jon. *The Time Warp Trio.* (Series). New York, NY: Viking.

Scieszka, Jon. *The True Story of the Three Little Pigs.* Illustrated by Lane Smith. New York, NY: Viking.

Selden, George. *The Cricket in Times Square.* (Series). New York, NY: Dell.

Sharmat, Marjorie Weinman. *Nate the Great.* (Series). New York, NY: Dell Yearling.

Smucker, Barbara. *Jacob's Little Giant.* Toronto, ON: Penguin Books.

Sobol, Donald J. *Encyclopedia Brown.* (Series). New York, NY: Bantam Skylark.

Warner, Gertrude Chandler. *The Boxcar Children.* (Series). New York, NY: Albert Whitman.

Wilson, Eric. *The Inuk Mountie Adventure.* (Series). Toronto, ON: HarperCollins.

69: Books for Fluent Readers

Atwater, Richard and Florence. *Mr. Popper's Penguins.* New York, NY: Dell.

Avi. *Poppy.* (Sequel: *Poppy and Rye.*) New York, NY: Avon.

Babbitt, Natalie. *Tuck Everlasting.* New York, NY: Bantam Skylark.

Byars, Betsy. *The Midnight Fox.* New York, NY: Puffin.

Byars, Betsy. *The Pinballs.* New York, NY: Harper Trophy.

Cleary, Beverly. *Dear Mr. Henshaw.* (Sequel: *Strider.*) New York, NY: William Morrow.

Cooper, Susan. *The Boggart.* (Sequel: *The Boggart and the Monster.*) New York, NY: Aladdin.

Curtis, Christopher Paul. *The Watsons Go To Birmingham - 1963.* New York, NY: Delacorte.

de Felice, Cynthia. *Weasel.* New York, NY: Macmillan.

Feiffer, Jules. *A Barrel of Laughs / A Vale of Tears.* New York, NY: HarperCollins.

Fleischman, Paul. *The Half-a-moon Inn.* New York, NY: Harper Trophy.

Fleischman, Sid. *The Whipping Boy.* New York, NY: William Morrow.

George, Jean Craighead. *Julie of the Wolves.* (Sequels: *Julie; Julie's Wolf Pack.*) New York, NY: HarperCollins.

Henkes, Kevin. *Words of Stone.* New York, NY: Puffin.

Hesse, Karen. *The Music of the Dolphins.* New York, NY: Scholastic.

Korman, Gordon. *The Chicken Doesn't Skate.* New York, NY: Scholastic.

Levine, Gail Carson. *Ella Enchanted.* New York, NY: HarperCollins.

Little, Jean. *Mama's Going to Buy You a Mockingbird.* Toronto, ON: Penguin.

Little, Jean. *The Belonging Place.* Toronto, ON: Penguin.

Lord, Bette Bao. *In the Year of the Boar and Jackie Robinson.* New York, NY: Harper Trophy.

Lottridge, Celia Barker. *Ticket to Curlew.* (Sequel: *Wings to Fly*.) Toronto, ON: Groundwood.

Lowry, Lois. *Anastasia Krupnik.* (Series). New York, NY: Bantam.

Lowry, Lois. *Number the Stars.* New York, NY: Bantam Doubleday Dell.

Lunn, Janet. *The Hollow Tree.* Toronto, ON: Knopf.

Meadowbooks: Level 5. Toronto, ON: Harcourt Brace.

Montgomery, L.M. *Anne of Green Gables.* (Series). New York, NY: Putnam.

Naylor, Phyllis Reynolds. *Shiloh.* (Sequels: *Shiloh Season; Saving Shiloh*.) New York, NY: Bantam Doubleday.

Norton, Mary. *The Borrowers.* (Series). San Diego, CA: Harcourt Brace Jovanovich.

Paterson, Katherine. *Bridge to Terabithia.* New York, NY: Crowell.

Paulsen, Gary. *Hatchet.* (Also: *The River; Brian's Winter*.) New York, NY: Puffin.

Pearson, Kit. *Awake and Dreaming.* Toronto, ON: Puffin.

Philbrick, Rodman. *Freak The Mighty.* (Sequel: *Max the Mighty*.) New York, NY: Scholastic.

Spinelli, Jerry. *Maniac Magee.* Boston, MA: Little Brown.

Steig, William. *Abel's Island.* New York, NY: Bantam Skylark.

Walters, Eric. *Trapped in Ice.* Toronto, ON: Viking.

White, Ruth. *Belle Prater's Boy.* New York, NY: Bantam Doubleday.

70: Books for Independent Readers

Alexander, Lloyd. *The Book of Three.* (Series). New York, NY: Dell.

Avi. *Nothing But The Truth.* New York, NY: Orchard.

Avi. *The True Confessions of Charlotte Doyle.* New York, NY: Orchard.

Burnett, Frances. *The Secret Garden.* New York, NY: Dell.

Christopher, John. *The White Mountains.* (Trilogy). New York, NY: Collier.

Cooper, Susan. *Over Sea, Under Stone.* (Series). London, UK: Puffin.

Creech, Sharon. *Walk Two Moons.* New York, NY: HarperCollins.

Cushman, Karen. *Catherine, Called Birdy.* New York, NY: Clarion.

Cushman, Karen. *The Midwife's Apprentice.* New York, NY: Houghton Mifflin.

Doyle, Brian. *Uncle Ronald.* Toronto, ON: Groundwood.

Farmer, Nancy. *A Girl Named Disaster.* New York, NY: Orchard.

Fine, Anne. *Flour Babies.* London, UK: Puffin.

Fitzhugh, Louise. *Nobody's Family is Going to Change.* New York, NY: Dell Yearling.

Hesse, Karen. *Out of the Dust.* New York, NY: Scholastic.

Holm, Anne. *I Am David.* London, UK: Methuen.

Holman, Felice. *Slake's Limbo.* New York, NY: Aladdin.

Hughes, Monica. *The Keeper of the Isis Light.* (Trilogy). Toronto, ON: Reed.

Jacques, Brian. *Redwall.* (Series). London, UK: Random House.

Johnston, Julie. *Hero of Lesser Causes.* Toronto, ON: Stoddart.

Konigsburg, E.L. *The View From Saturday.* New York, NY: Atheneum.

L'Engle, Madelaine. *A Wrinkle in Time.* (Trilogy). New York, NY: Dell.

Little, Jean. *Listen for the Singing.* Toronto, ON: Clark Irwin.

Lowry, Lois. *The Giver.* Boston, MA: Houghton Mifflin.

Lunn, Janet. *Shadow on Hawthorn Bay.* Toronto, ON: Lester and Orpen Dennys.

Meadowbooks, Level 6. Toronto, ON: Harcourt Brace.

O'Brien, Robert C. *Mrs. Frisby and the Rats of NIMH.* New York, NY: Atheneum.

Oppel, Kenneth. *Silverwing.* Toronto, ON: HarperCollins.

Paterson, Katherine. *JIP: His Story.* New York, NY: Crowell.

Paulsen, Gary. *The Monument.* New York, NY: Orchard.

Paulsen, Gary. *The Rifle.* San Diego, CA: Harcourt Brace.

Paulsen, Gary. *The Transall Saga.* New York, NY: Delacorte.

Pullman, Philip. *The Golden Compass.* (Trilogy). New York, NY: Ballantine.

Sachar, Louis. *Holes.* New York, NY: Farrar, Straus and Giroux.

Spinelli, Jerry. *Wringer.* New York, NY: HarperCollins.

Taylor, Mildred. *Roll of Thunder Hear My Cry*. New York, NY: Dial.

Waugh, Sylvia. *The Mennyms*. (Series). London, UK: Red Fox.

Wynne-Jones, Tim. *The Maestro*. Toronto, ON: Groundwood.

71: Books for Reading Aloud

Aska, Warabé and David Day. *Aska's Sea Creatures*. Toronto, ON: Doubleday.

Barton, Bob. *The Best and Dearest Chick of All*. Illustrated by Coral Nault. Red Deer, AB: Northern Lights.

Barton, Bob. *The Storm Wife*. Kingston, ON: Quarry.

Baylor, Byrd. *I'm In Charge of Celebrations*. New York, NY: Charles Scribner and Sons.

Bierhorst, John. (ed.). *The Dancing Fox: Arctic Folktales*. Illustrated by Mary Kokheena. New York, NY: William Morrow.

Bogart, Jo Ellen and Laura Fernandez. *Jeremiah Learns to Read*. Illustrated by Rick Jacobson. Toronto, ON: North Winds.

Booth, David. *The Dust Bowl*. Illustrated by Karen Reczuch. Toronto, ON: Kids Can.

Booth, David. *Til All The Stars Have Fallen*. Toronto, ON: Kids Can.

Bunting, Eve. *I Am The Mummy Heb-Nefert*. San Diego, CA: Harcourt Brace.

Chimo, Shirley. *Treasure of Princesses*. New York, NY: HarperCollins

Coerr, Eleanor. *Sadako*. New York, NY: Putnam.

Davis, Aubrey. *Bone Button Borscht*. Toronto, ON: Kids Can.

Davis, Aubrey. *The Enormous Potato*. Toronto, ON: Kids Can.

Denim, Sue and Dav Pilkey. *The Dumb Bunnies*. (Series). New York, NY: Scholastic.

Doval, Marguerite. *Paper Dragon*. New York, NY: Atheneum.

Ehlert, Lois. *Cukoo*. San Diego, CA: Harcourt Brace.

Gal, Laszlo and Raffaille. *The Parrot*. Toronto, ON: Groundwood Books.

Gay, Marie Louise. *Rumplestiltskin*. Toronto, ON: Groundwood.

Ginsburg, Mirra. *Clay Bowl*. Illustrated by Jos. A. Smith. New York, NY: Greenwillow.

Hoffman, Mary. *Amazing Grace*. Illustrated by Caroline Burch. New York, NY: Dial.

Jarrell, Randall. *The Bat Poet*. (Also: *The Animal Family*.) New York, ON: HarperCollins.

Kennedy, Richard. *Collected Stories*. Illustrated by Marcia Sewall. New York, NY: Harper & Row

Kimmel, Eric. *Hershel and the Hanukkah Goblins*. New York, NY: Holiday House.

Lawson, Julie. *The Dragon's Pearl*. New York, NY: Clarion.

Lionni, Leo. *Frederick's Fables*. New York, NY: Pantheon.

Lottridge, Celia Barker. *Ten Small Tales*. Illustrated by Joanna Fitzgerald. Toronto, ON: Groundwood Books.

Martin, Jr., Bill, and John Archambault. *The Ghost-Eye Tree*. Illustrated by Ted Rand. New York, NY: Henry Holt.

Martin, Eva. *Canadian Fairy Tales*. Toronto, ON: Douglas and MacIntyre.

Mills, Lauren. *The Rag Coat*. Boston, MA: Little Brown.

Polacco, Patricia. *Thank You, Mr. Falker*. New York, NY: Philomel.

Ringgold, Faith. *Tar Beach*. New York, NY: Crown.

San Souci, Robert D. *Sootface: An Objibwa Cinderella Story*. Illustrated by Daniel San Souci. New York, NY: Bantam Doubleday.

Shannon, David. *A Bad Case of the Stripes*. New York, NY: Scholastic.

Steptoe, John. *Mufaro's Beautiful Daughters*. New York, NY: Lothrop Lee and Shepard.

Van Laan, Nancy. *In A Circle Long Ago*. Illustrated by Lisa Desimini. New York, NY: Knopf.

Wallace, Ian. *Hansel and Gretel*. Toronto, ON: Groundwood Books.

Whetung, James. *The Vision Seeker*. Illustrated by Paul Morin. Toronto, ON: Stoddart.

White, E.B. *Charlotte's Web*. New York, NY: Harper & Row.

Yashinsky, Dan. *The Storyteller at Fault*. Illustrated by Nancy Cairine Pitt. Charlottetown, PEI: Ragweed.

Yee, Paul. *Tales From Gold Mountain*. Toronto, ON: Groundwood.

Yolen, Jane. *Owl Moon*. New York, NY: Philomel.

Young, Ed. *Lon Po Po: A Red Riding Hood Story From China*. New York, NY: Philomel.

Zelinsky, Paul O. *Rapunzel*. New York, NY: Dutton.

72: Books for Shared Reading

1. Repetition of Words, Phrases, Stanzas, Refrains, Dialogues

Brown, Margaret Wise. *Goodnight Moon*. Illustrated by Clement Hurd. New York, NY: HarperCollins.

Browne, Anthony. *I Like Books*. New York, NY: Knopf.

Carle, Eric. *The Very Quiet Cricket*. New York, NY: Philomel.

Clarke, Gus. *EiEiO*. London, UK: Red Fox.

Fox, Mem. *Tough Boris*. Illustrated by Kathryn Brown. San Diego, CA: Harcourt Brace.

Wood, Audrey. *Silly Sally*. San Diego, CA: Harcourt Brace.

2. Rhythm and Rhyme

Baker, Keith. *Who Is the Beast?* San Diego, CA: Harcourt Brace.

Baker, Keith. *Hide and Snake*. San Diego, CA: Harcourt Brace.

Fox, Mem. *Time for Bed*. San Diego, CA: Harcourt Brace.

Kellogg, Steven. *A-Hunting We Will Go*. New York, NY: Morrow Junior Books.

Seuss, Dr. *Green Eggs and Ham*. New York, NY: Random House.

3. Cumulative Sequence Pattern

Aardema, Verna. *Bringing the Rain to Kapiti Plain*. New York, NY: Dial Books.

Aardema, Verna. *Why Mosquitoes Buzz in People's Ears*. New York, NY: Pied Piper.

Martin, Bill Jr. *Old Devil Wind*. San Diego, CA: Harcourt Brace.

Taback, Simms. *There Was an Old Lady Who Swallowed a Fly*. New York, NY: Penguin.

Wood, Audrey. *The Napping House*. Illustrated by Don Wood. San Diego, CA: Harcourt Brace.

4. Interlocking Sequences

Hutchins, Pat. *The Doorbell Rang*. New York, NY: Greenwillow.

Pienkowski. Jan. *Gossip*. Los Angeles, CA: Price/Stern/Sloan.

Stevenson, James. *It Could Be Worse*. New York, NY: Greenwillow.

Williams, Linda. *The Old Lady Who Was Not Afraid of Anything*. New York, NY: Crowell.

5. Cultural Sequences

Garne, S.T. *One White Sail — A Caribbean Counting Book*. New York, NY: Simon and Schuster.

Hutchins, Pat. *1 Hunter*. New York, NY: Greenwillow.

Lottridge, Celia Barker. *One Watermelon Seed*. Illustrated by Karen Patkai. Toronto, ON: Oxford.

Manning, Linda. *Animal Hours*. Illustrated by Vlastra van Kampen. Toronto, ON: Stoddart.

Martin, Bill Jr. and Archambault, Jon. *Chicka Chicka Boom Boom*. Illustrated by Lois Ehlert. New York, NY: Henry Holt.

Shannon, George. *Tomorrow's Alphabet*. Illustrated by Donald Crews. New York, NY: Greenwillow.

Van Allsburg, Chris. *The Z Was Zapped: A Play in Twenty-Six Acts*. Boston, MA: Houghton Mifflin.

6. Opposites

Bauer, Caroline Feller. *My Mom Travels A Lot*. Illustrated by Nancy Winslow Parker. New York, NY: Puffin.

Stevenson, James. *Fun!/No Fun!* New York, NY: Greenwillow.

Stinson, Kathy. *Big or Little*. Toronto, ON: Annick.

Wood, Audrey. *Piggies*. Illustrated by Don Wood. San Diego, CA: Harcourt Brace.

7. Comparisons

Barrett, Judi. *Things That Are Most in the World*. Illustrated by John Nickle. New York, NY: Atheneum.

Lyon, George Ella. *Together*. Illustrated by Vera Rosenberry. New York, NY: Orchard Books.

Wood, Audrey. *Quick as a Cricket*. Illustrated by Don Wood. New York, NY: Child's Play.

8. Problem and Resolution

Demers, Jan. *On Sunday I Lost My Cat*. Illustrated by Estella Hickman. New York, NY: Riverwood.

Lloyd, David. *The Sneeze*. Illustrated by Fritz Wegner. London, UK: Walker Books.

Most, Bernard. *Whatever Happened to the Dinosaurs?* San Diego, CA: Harcourt Brace.

9. Cause and Effect

Brown, Ruth. *The Big Sneeze*. Toronto, ON: Stoddart.

Gilman, Phoebe. *Something from Nothing*. Richmond Hill, ON: North Winds.

Greene, Carol. *The Old Ladies Who Liked Cats*. Illustrated by Loretta Krupinski. New York, NY: HarperCollins.

Rosen, Michael. *We're Going on a Bear Hunt*. Illustrated by Helen Oxenbury. London, UK: Walker Books.

Silverstein, Shel. *The Giving Tree*. New York, NY: HarperCollins.

Stevenson, James. *Quick! Turn the Page*. New York, NY: Greenwillow.

10. Syntactic Structure

Allen, Pamela. *Fancy That!* New York, NY: Penguin.

Brown, Ruth. *A Dark, Dark Tale*. New York, NY: Scholastic.

Hoberman, Mary Ann. *A House Is a House for Me*. New York, NY: Penguin.

Lester, Alison. *Rosie Sips Spiders*. Boston, MA: Houghton Mifflin.

Most, Bernard. *The Cow That Went Oink*. San Diego, CA: Harcourt Brace.

11. Story Shapes

Ahlberg, Allan and Janet. *Funnybones*. London, UK: Heinemann.

Beck, Ian. *Little Miss Muffett*. Oxford, UK: Oxford Press.

Burningham, John. *Where's Julius?* London, UK: Random House.

Little, Jean and De Vries, Maggie. *Once Upon a Golden Apple*. Illustrated by Phoebe Gilman, Markham, ON: Viking.

12. Question and Answer

Carlstrom, Nancy White. *Goodbye Geese*. Illustrated by Ed Young. New York, NY: Putnam.

Mazer, Anne. *The Salamander Room*. Illustrated by Steve Johnson. New York, NY: Knopf.

Shaw, Charles G. *It Looks Like Spilt Milk*. New York, NY: Harper & Row.

Williams, Sue. *I Went Walking*. Illustrated by Julie Vivas. San Diego, CA: Harcourt Brace.

Zolotow, Charlotte. *When The Wind Stops*. Illustrated by Stefano Vitale. New York, NY: HarperCollins.

13. Chronological Order

Aliki. *At Mary Bloom's*. New York, NY: Greenwillow.

Carle, Eric, *The Very Hungry Caterpillar*. New York, NY: Putnam.

Numeroff, Laura. *If You Give a Moose a Muffin*. Illustrated by Felicia Bond. New York, NY: HarperCollins.

73: Software Resources and Internet Addresses

CD-ROMs

These CD-ROMs are excellent examples of motivating materials. Some are interactive stories, some are exciting information resources, some are tools that promote creativity. This is a very short list of CD-ROMs from among many you could find to promote literacy in children.

Amazing Animals Activity Pack
Level: ECE-3

Almost any Dorling Kindersley CD-ROM is worth buying! The Amazing Animals CD-ROM is no exception. Twenty different activities involving animals are included, from taking a photo safari to identifying animal sounds. The graphics and sounds can be exported to other applications.

Being a Scientist
Level: J/I

Children help solve the mystery of the vanishing trees by finding clues and testing scientific ideas as they navigate their way around the forest through the village to the town, develop skills of investigation, observation, and deduction, and focus on curriculum outcomes normally difficult to achieve in a classroom. The CD-ROM includes Internet links.

Cetaenia: A Journey through the World of Whales, Dolphins and Porpoises
Level: J

This CD-ROM comprises *Waiting for the Whales* read by the author, information on over thirty species of cetaceans, video footage, interactive interviews with scientists and researchers, Internet simulation, hot links to real Internet sites, teacher's guide, and blackline masters.

Crossword Magic
Level: All

This is a new, jazzier version of the old classic with color and manual editing. It is easy enough for any child to create crosswords.

Diary Maker
Level: 4 and Up

A multimedia diary-making tool that contains three diaries to explore as powerful examples: Anne Frank, Zlata Filipovic, and Latoya Hunter. Children are encouraged to be creative, expressive, and reflective. This CD-ROM is an excellent example of a useful educational multimedia package.

Earth Explorer
Level: J/I

This multimedia encyclopedia of the environment includes an interactive tour of the planet, facts about the world we live in, a multitude of articles with visual and multimedia displays by many environmentalists and artists, games and activities on a variety of issues, and interactive data displays. The CD-ROM makes children aware of cause and effect in relation to what we do to the earth.

Field Trip to the Sky
Level: Late P/J/I

This is a fun, easy-to-use program that allows users to explore the brilliance and magnitude of space while navigating through the solar system. It contains a multimedia encyclopedia, a visual database of the latest NASA pictures and videos, interactive laboratories, and a challenging game.

Hyperstudio
Level: All Ages

This program lets students from grade one to university create multimedia, hypermedia presentations with their own graphics, clip art, video clips, writing, voices, recorded sounds, and more.

Juillard Music Adventure
Level: J/I

With music recorded by real Juillard students, this CD-ROM takes children through a series of puzzles to solve a mystery in a castle. Along the way, they learn the elements of pitch, rhythm, melody, and meter at three levels of difficulty. Children may even compose and save simple scores!

Kids Media Magic
Level: PreK-4

This package encourages reading and writing, and includes over 400 rebus vocabulary words with pictures and recorded speech, text-to-speech and sound recording, an integrated paint program, and publishing options.

Kid Pix Studio Deluxe
Level: All Ages

This CD-ROM, which has simple animation, is a creativity tool that allows children from 3 to 103 write stories, create graphics, add clip art, and record their voice to make picture books or slide-show presentations.

Learning to Read on the Promenade
Level: K

Young children can use this interactive early learning software to have fun as they practise sound skills, including rhyming words, read along with stories, and take part in creative activities such as making cards, letters, or pictures.

Living Books
Level: ECE-4

Volume One includes the following stories: *Just Grandma and Me, Arthur's Teacher Trouble, The New Kid on the Block, Tortoise and the Hare*; Volume Two includes the following stories: *Little Monster at School, Arthur's Birthday, Harry and the Haunted House, The Berenstein Bears Get in a Fight. Green Eggs and Ham* is on its own CD ROM and contains many prereading and reading activities.

Mieko: A Story of Japanese Culture
Level: P/J, /I/S

This excellent Broderbund CD-ROM, based on the story by Leo Politi, takes children through Mieko's discovery of her culture in English, French, Japanese, Spanish, or German. Extra activities include making an origami crane, and learning various aspects of the Japanese culture. The disk includes narration, photos, graphics, and a photo tour of Japan.

My City
Level: J/I

Developed by UNICEF, this multicultural CD-ROM explores many of the issues faced by a "mayor" as she or he tries to run a city in a responsible way. Some of the issues include poverty, pollution, drugs, vandalism, health care, and much more. Every issue has four viewpoints. The disk has a great deal of information about issues around the world.

Old MacDonald Had a Farm
Level: K-2

The graphics, animation, video, and music will charm young learners as they explore the farm, learn about food from around the world, practise listening and reading along, and take part in singing activities. There is an integrated paint program and farm clip art that children can use to create their own farm images. Also included are printable song sheets and skill worksheets.

Print Artist 4.0 Platinum
Level: All

This tool includes a multitude of graphics, typefaces, and professionally designed layouts, as well as offering photo enhancement and morphing. Create a business, keep budgets, write reports, design stationery, and take part in any form of publishing venture with this powerful tool.

Putt-Putt Travels Through Time
Level: ECE/P

An excellent starting point for software for young children. The curious little cat Putt-Putt, takes children on adventures through time to visit dinosaurs, Mediaeval Times, the Old West, and the future!

Sky Island Mysteries
Level: Late P/J/I

The latest in the Thinkin' Things series, this CD-ROM poses fourteen challenging mysteries with hundreds of critical-thinking challenges. Children can practice observation, reading, listening, prioritizing, and reasoning skills as they solve the puzzles.

SPY Fox in Dry Cereal
Level: P/J

Challenge kids to be problem solvers with this adventure mystery. Cows are cownapped. Children must question suspects, crack codes, and explore the countryside while attempting to solve the mystery.

Strategy Games of the World
Level: Late P/J/I

Play Mancala and Nine Man's Morris, games that have challenged people for thousands of years. Children learn strategies that transfer to all areas

of learning (and life!). Many levels of skills. Strategy coach gives tips and alternative strategies. There are even videos showing how these strategies might apply to real life.

What's the Secret? Volume 2
Level: Late P/J/I

Answers to questions kids ask! "How does a plane get off the ground?", Why does glue stick?" If you want your students to pose questions, this CD ROM is for you. This volume addresses the Arctic, the brain, flight and glue.

World Wildlife Atlas
Level: J/I/S

Use a map of the world to zoom into any geopolitical, or environmental area, then select the wildlife from that area. Pictures and videos help children learn about the world's animals.

Internet Sites

Here is a brief selection from among the thousands of excellent Internet sites that will have children reading, writing, and engaging in a multitude of activities.

http://db.cochran.com/li_toc:theoPage.db

This is a list of best sites for children! Each site has been carefully selected, reviewed, and given a rating out of five. The site contains a number of connections to other wonderful sites that young children (3-8) and their parents can visit, including the Interactive Theodore Tugboat stories where children can choose their own endings to stories; Spiderman adventure stories, rebuses, and puzzles, Berenstein Bear activities, and much more.

http://www.tc.cornell.edu/Kids.on.Campus/WWWDemo/

This is a wonderful page for 7-to-12 year olds with links to science topics such as space, dinosaurs, disasters, and weather. It includes problem-solving activities, a magazine, and links to a host of excellent sites.

http://www.kidlib.org/kidopedia/

Located in the Queen's University Site, this is an encyclopedia written by children for children. The exciting part of this site is that children may submit articles to be added to the "kidopedia." Some selections are in other languages – children can be encouraged to read them to practise second or third languages.

http://www.schoolnet.ca/english/arts/lit/c-voice/
This site publishes children's writing from JK to grade 8 and helps to guide those who wish to share their, or their students', writing with others. There are many samples of stories by children that can be read aloud or shared with the class. The site contains guidelines regarding parental permission and anonymity, which are important when publishing children's work of any kind. The information can be obtained in French or English.

http://webs.coled.umn.edu/schools/Maps/Canada.html
This site shows a map of Canada. A click on one of the provinces, and all the schools that have registered with webs are listed in alphabetical order. Children can learn about Canadian schools, read projects others have completed, and check out the interesting local links many schools provide with their sites. This is a wonderful resource for those involved in setting up a web page for themselves or their school. By reviewing each site, they can begin to discern what makes a site good/weak and incorporate positive elements in their site.

http://www.npac.syr.edu/textbook/kidsweb/
The goal of Kid's Web is to present children with a subset of the Web that is simple to navigate, and contains information targeted at the K-12 level. Each subject section, as depicted by the buttons, contains a list of links to understandable, interesting information. There are also links to external lists of material on each subject, which older children can review for further information.

http://www.sas.upenn.edu/African_Studies/Home_Page/AFR_GID E.html
This wonderful site is chuck full of information for children who are fascinated by Africa. It includes aspects of the continent's history, geography, and folklore. As well, it includes short stories written by other children and current events coverage written to appeal to children. There are excellent links to a wide variety of resources.

http://www.exploratorium.edu/
Children can learn about memory, discover what facial features are the most important in a disguise, guess the famous face in the Elvis wig, build a 'glitter globe,' discover the science of various sports, and much more.

http://sln.fi.edu/qa98/qanda5.html
Supported by the Franklin Institute, this site identifies new and interesting Net activities for kids. There are five immediate links. The first, Spotlighting, comprises the results of a field trip taken by a group of classes in a Pennsylvania school as children research the delicate ocean ecosystem. Their experiments, writing, and photos highlight this link. Other links include mazes, math activities, music, stories, arts and crafts, and dissections done by a group of students along with pictures. This site will fascinate children eight years of age and older.

http://www.comlab.ox.ac.uk/archive/other/museums/world.html
This site provides links to museums all over the world. Children can choose a country to visit, then a section of the country, then the museums in that vicinity. Many of the museums have virtual tours with descriptions and search engines that a child can use to learn more about a favorite area.

http://fromnowon.org/museum/list.html
An interesting site that guides children to museums built by other children. Sites include a museum built by grade 4/5 students about their community, including information about famous members (as selected by the children), special school and community events, regional geography, a history of the community, and other topics.

http://www.pomona.edu/visual-lit/intro/intro.html
This is an interesting site for the budding young artist. Children from ten and up will enjoy reading and trying out this learning site on what dots, lines, shapes, and so on mean in relation to art. There are video clips to illustrate each concept.

http://fox.nstn.ca/puppets/activity.html
This site comprises a wonderful page with links to others that focus on making puppets, reading puppet plays by other children, submitting plays for Internet publication, writing well, and much more.

http://www.worldvillage.com/famsite.html
The Family Site-of-the-Day was created to highlight web sites that produce quality content appropriate for family viewing and participation. A new site is highlighted each day!

Teachers and children will find links to sites about women scientists and equity issues. There are equally wonderful "how to" step-by-step lessons that children from 10 to 100 will be able to follow to try new, interesting math activities.

74: Professional References

Adams, Marilyn Jager, Barbara R. Foorman, Ingvar Lundberg, and Terri Beeler. *Phonemic Awareness in Young Children*. Baltimore, MD: Paul H. Brookes Publishing, 1998.

Allen, Janet, and Kyle Gonzalez. *There's Room For Me Here: Literacy Workshop in the Middle School*. York, ME: Stenhouse Publishers, 1998.

Anthony, Robert J., Terry D. Johnson, Norma I. Mickelson, and Alison Preece. *Evaluating Literacy: A Perspective for Change*. Toronto, ON: Irwin Publishing, 1991.

Atwell, Nancie. *In the Middle: New Understandings About Writing, Reading, and Learning*. 2nd ed. Portsmouth, NH: Heinemann; Toronto, ON: Irwin Publishing, 1998.

Barton, Bob, and David Booth. *Stories in the Classroom: Storytelling, Reading Aloud, and Roleplaying with Children*. Markham, ON: Pembroke Publishers, 1990.

Baskwill, Jane. *Parents and Teachers: Partners in Learning*. Toronto, ON: Scholastic, 1989.

Benton, Michael, and Geoff Fox. *Teaching Literature: Nine to Fourteen*. Oxford, UK: Oxford University Press, 1985.

Bialostok, Steven. *Raising Readers: Helping Your Child to Literacy*. Winnipeg, MB: Peguis Publishers, 1992.

Binkley, Marilyn R. *Becoming a Nation of Readers: What Parents Can Do*. Indianapolis, IN: D.C. Heath, 1988.

Booth, David, Jack Booth, Jo Phenix, and Doreen Scott-Dunne. *Word Sense: Level A,B,C*. Toronto, ON: Harcourt Brace, 1994.

Booth, David, Jack Booth, Jo Phenix, and Doreen Scott-Dunne. *Word Sense: Level 4,5,6*. Toronto, ON: Harcourt Brace, 1996.

Booth, David, Larry Swartz, and Meguido Zola. *Choosing Children's Books*. Markham, ON: Pembroke Publishers, 1987.

Booth, David, ed. *Literacy Techniques for Building Successful Readers and Writers*. Markham, ON: Pembroke Publishers, 1996.

Booth, David. *Classroom Voices: Language-Based Learning in the Elementary School*. Toronto, ON: Harcourt Brace, 1994.

Calkins, Lucy McCormick. *Living Between the Lines*. Portsmouth, NH: Heinemann; Toronto: Irwin Publishing, 1991.

Calkins, Lucy McCormick. *Raising Lifelong Learners: A Parent's Guide*. Reading, MA: Addison-Wesley, 1997.

Chambers, Aidan. *Tell Me: Children, Reading, and Talk*. York, ME: Stenhouse Publishers; Markham, ON: Pembroke Publishers, 1996.

Clay, Dame Marie M. *The Early Detection of Reading Difficulties*. 3rd ed. Auckland, NZ: Heinemann, 1979.

Coles, Gerald. *Reading Lessons: The Debate Over Literacy*. New York, NY: Hill and Wang, 1998.

Cullinan, Bernice E. *Let's Read About: Finding Books They'll Love to Read*. Toronto, ON: Scholastic, 1993.

Daniels, Harvey. *Literature Circles: Voice and Choice in the Student-Centered Classroom*. York, ME: Stenhouse Publishers; Markham, ON: Pembroke Publishers, 1994.

Derewianka, Beverly. *Exploring How Texts Work*. Newtown, Australia: Primary English Teaching Association, 1990.

Devers III, William J., and James Cipielewski. *Every Teacher's Thematic Booklist*. Richmond Hill, ON: Scholastic, 1993.

Dombey, Henrietta, Margaret Moustafa, et. al. *Whole to Part Phonics: How Children Learn to Read and Spell*. London, UK: Centre for Language in Primary Education, 1998.

Donavin, Denise Perry. ed. *Best of the Best for Children*. New York, NY: Random House, 1992.

Fountas, Irene C., and Gay Su Pinnell. *Guided Reading: Good First Teaching for All Children*. Portsmouth, NH: Heinemann, 1996.

Fry, Edward Bernard, Jacqueline E. Kress, and Dona Lee Fountoukidis. *The Reading Teacher's Book of Lists*. 3rd ed. Englewood Cliffs, NJ: Prentice Hall, 1993.

Goodman, Ken. *On Reading: A Common-sense Look at the Nature of Language and the Science of Reading*. Richmond Hill, ON: Scholastic, 1996.

Goodman, Ken. *Phonics Phacts: A Common-sense Look at the Most Controversial Issue Affecting Today's Classrooms!* Richmond Hill, ON: Scholastic, 1993.

Graves, Donald H., and Bonnie S. Sunstein. eds. *Portfolio Portraits.* Toronto, ON: Irwin Publishing, 1992.

Hart-Hewins, Linda, and Jan Wells. *Read It in the Classroom! Organizing an Interactive Language Arts Program Grades 4-9.* Markham, ON: Pembroke Publishers, 1992.

Harvey, Stephanie. *Nonfiction Matters: Reading, Writing, and Research in Grades 3-8.* York, ME: Stenhouse Publishers, 1998.

Hayhoe, Mike, and Stephen Parker. *Working with Fiction.* London, UK: Edward Arnold, 1984.

Heide, Ann, and Linda Stilborne. *The Teacher's Guide to the Internet.* Toronto, ON: Trifolium Books, 1996.

Hindley, Joanne. *In The Company of Children.* York, ME: Stenhouse Publishers, 1996.

Hughes, Margaret, and Dennis Searle. *The Violent E and Other Tricky Sounds: Learning to Spell from Kindergarten Through Grade 6.* York, ME: Stenhouse Publishers; Markham, ON: Pembroke Publishers, 1997.

Jobe, Ron, and Paula Hart. *Canadian Connections: Experiencing Literature with Children.* Markham, ON: Pembroke Publishers, 1991.

Johnston, Peter H. *Knowing Literacy: Constructive Literacy Assessment.* York, ME: Stenhouse Publishers, 1997.

Leu, Jr., Donald J., and Deborah Diadiun Leu. *Teaching with the Internet: Lessons from the Classroom.* Norwood, AUS: Christopher-Gordon Publishers, 1997.

Ministry of Education, Ontario. *Assessing Language Arts.* Toronto, ON: Queen's Printer of Ontario, 1990.

Moustafa, Margaret. *Beyond Traditional Phonics: Research Discoveries and Reading Instruction.* Portsmouth, NH: Heinemann, 1997.

New Zealand Ministry of Education. *Reading for Life: The Learner as a Reader.* Wellington, NZ: Learning Media Limited, 1996.

Peterson, Ralph, and Maryann Eeds. *Grand Conversations: Literature Groups in Action.* Richmond Hill, ON: Scholastic, 1990.

Phenix, Jo. *The Spelling Teacher's Book of Lists: Words to Illustrate Spelling Patterns...And Tips for Teaching Them.* Markham, ON: Pembroke Publishers, 1996.

Phinney, Margaret Yatsevitch. *Reading With the Troubled Reader.* Richmond Hill, ON: Scholastic, 1988.

Rasinski, Timothy, and Nancy Padak. *Holistic Reading Strategies: Teaching Children Who Find Reading Difficult.* Englewood Cliffs, NJ: Merrill, 1996.

Robinson, Anne, Leslie Crawford, and Nigel Hall. *Someday You Will No All About Me: Young Children's Explorations in the World of Letters.* Markham, ON: Pembroke Publishers, 1991.

Routman, Regie. *Invitations: Changing as Teachers and Learners K-12.* Portsmouth, NH: Heinemann; Toronto, ON: Irwin Publishing, 1994.

Schwartz, Susan, and Maxine Bone. *Retelling, Relating, Reflecting: Beyond the 3 R's.* Toronto, ON: Irwin Publishing, 1995.

Strube, Penny. *Getting the Most from Literature Groups.* Toronto, ON: Scholastic Professional Books, 1996.

Swartz, Larry, and David Booth. *Novel Sense, Level 4,5,6.* Toronto, ON: Harcourt Brace, 1997.

Thompson, Jack. *Understanding Teenagers' Reading: Reading Processes and the Teaching of Literature.* New York, NY: Nichols Publishing, 1987.

Thomson, Jack, ed. *Reconstructing Literature Teaching: New Essays on the Teaching of Literature.* Norwood, AUS: Australian Association for the Teaching of English, 1992.

Vopat, James. *The Parent Project: A Workshop Approach to Parent Involvement.* York, ME: Stenhouse Publishers, 1994.

Waring, Cynthia Conway. *Developing Independent Readers: Strategy-Oriented Reading Activities for Learners with Special Needs.* West Nyack, NY: The Center for Applied Research in Education, 1995.

Weaver, Constance, Lorraine Gillmeister-Krause, and Grace Vento-Zogby. *Creating Support for Effective Literacy Education.* Portsmouth, NH: Heinemann, 1996.

Wells, Gordon, et. al. *Changing Schools From Within: Creating Communities of Inquiry.* Toronto, ON: OISE Press, 1994.

Wells, Jan, and Linda Hart-Hewins. *Phonics Too! How To Teach Skills in a Balanced Language Program.* Markham, ON: Pembroke Publishers, 1994.

Wolf, Dennie Palmer, and Julie Craven, eds. *More Than the Truth: Teaching Nonfiction Writing Through Journalism.* Portsmouth, NH: Heinemann, 1996.

Yopp, Hallie Kay, and Ruth Helen Yopp. *Literature-Based Reading Activities.* 2nd ed. Toronto, ON: Allyn and Bacon, 1996.

Appendix:
Checklists, Guidelines, and Rubrics

Reading Outcomes

The following outcomes represent some of the issues, skills, concepts, and strategies that we can examine when assessing a child's reading development.

1. A child who is involved with books and other print resources:
- is aware of a variety of reading materials in the language arts classroom, in other curriculum areas, at home (e.g., books, environmental print, computers, magazines)
- is aware of the characteristics of a variety of forms of text (e.g., letters, diaries, advertisements, novels, reference books)
- listens to and appreciates literature read aloud (at home, at school, live, taped)
- responds emotionally to text (appreciates humor, sadness etc.)
- has books on hand, owns books, or visits the library
- has a positive attitude toward reading (at home and in school)
- chooses books that are appropriate to ability and interest (e.g., number of pages, size of print, format, ratio of dialogue to narrative etc.)
- selects books by browsing, reading the first few pages, etc.
- selects books for satisfaction and enjoyment
- rereads favorite books
- reads during free time
- reads and writes outside of school
- reads increasingly greater amounts
- discusses reading experiences with those who have read and those who want to read the book
- looks for favorite authors and illustrators
- reads with little encouragement from others

2. A child who is demonstrating successful reading behavior:
- knows where to begin reading
- reads from left to right
- reads from top to bottom of a page
- returns to the left to start a new line of text
- knows the letters of the alphabet
- identifies the title and the author
- checks that pictures correspond to the meaning made with the text
- checks that words read aloud correspond to the meaning made from text
- can match sounds to letters while reading
- can match each spoken word to a written word
- applies the knowledge of the sounds of speech to reading
- uses clusters of letters to analyze a word
- looks for patterns of letters in words to represent sound and meaning
- identifies how words are similar
- uses known words to identify unknown words
- recognizes rhyming words
- uses more than one strategy to determine an unknown word
- reads on to the end of the line when meeting a difficult word
- has a basic sight vocabulary of known words
- approximates the meaning of a difficult word
- uses syntactic cues to identify function words

- uses context as a clue for understanding an unknown word
- recognizes multiple meanings of a word
- rereads a word, sentence, or passage to confirm meaning
- can explain how a new word was identified
- uses meaning and visual information to predict an unknown word
- puts in order a text that has been cut up into words
- writes new words using phonics cues
- uses correct consonants when spelling a word
- focuses on vowel sounds when spelling a word
- checks written work for errors
- solves unfamiliar words and concepts while reading
- reads for meaning
- self-monitors while reading
- uses substitution when confronting a difficult word
- confirms that substitutions make sense
- self-corrects when reading aloud
- continues to develop a storehouse of reading strategies
- problem solves new words or sentence patterns
- asks for help when needed from peers, teacher, and print references
- reads in a variety of situations, including individually, with a partner, in a small group, as a member of the classroom community
- can analyze the strategies that were used in reading a text
- reads aloud with phrasing and fluency
- is in control of personal reading growth
- reads independently and with confidence
- can read intensively for an appropriate period of time
- returns easily to a text after a time away
- reads books with increasingly difficult words, ideas, and structures
- knows when to continue or when to stop reading a difficult book

3. A child who is making connections to text:
- demonstrates sustained engagement with text
- understands the main point of the story
- predicts and confirms events in a story
- relates emotionally to characters and events, ideas and concepts
- compares information from one book to that of another
- can retell a story using words and phrases from the text
- relates information from the text to personal experience
- gives opinions about characters, their actions and beliefs
- relates a text to similar texts
- looks for meaning in text and pictures
- questions the information and the implications in a text to make the most meaning
- understands stated and unstated events in the story
- participates in discussions about reading, commenting on and listening to the ideas of peers
- confirms and clarifies ideas by referring to the text, quoting relevant points when possible
- changes opinions and beliefs, modifies viewpoint
- moves beyond summarizing a plot to significant responses to the whole text
- compares the work of various authors and genres
- recognizes text patterns inherent in a genre
- creates other forms of literature to demonstrate understanding and interpretation of a text
- identifies and articulates the author's purpose for writing

- participates in shared reading experiences
- shows personal involvement when talking about reading in conferences, and in journal writing

4. A child who understands the art of reading:
- examines the ways in which authors present ideas in texts
- reads critically and without bias
- knows how different text structures work
- uses the parts of a book to locate information
- is developing knowledge of how elements of a text works
- reads a variety of fiction and non-fiction texts
- identifies favorite genres, favorite authors
- reads at variable speeds to skim and scan for information
- rereads for clarification or for pleasure
- seeks meaning in a text different from personal experience
- discusses elements of a story, including characters, setting, time period, plot, mood, and structure
- appreciates how knowledge of literature can contribute to personal development
- appreciates how literature reflects and extends the aspects of a culture
- constructs meaning from a variety of texts, written for different purposes
- chooses to read some texts aloud with effective interpretive skills
- uses techniques and words drawn from the text when writing
- appreciates books as a positive and enriching influence
- continues to develop as a self-motivated lifelong reader and writer
- values personal reading achievements and those of others

Reading Interest and Attitude Inventory

You can create your own sets of inventories to use throughout the year from these suggestions.

1. How did you learn to read?
2. How would you describe yourself as a reader?
3. Do you know what kinds of books your friends like?
4. Do you know someone in your class who is a really good reader?
5. Suppose you had a penpal in the same grade in a different school and you wanted to find out about him or her as a reader. What questions would you ask?
6. Do you find some reading material harder than others? Can you give some examples? What makes one book harder than another?
7. Do you discuss books with the other kids?
8. What did you do in your reading time today?
9. How did you choose the book you are reading?
10. If I were listening to others talk about the book you're reading, what comments do you think I would hear?
11. Do you like to read?
12. When do you read?
13. Where do you read?
14. Do you ever buy books? What kind?
15. Do you read magazines?
16. Do you get a newspaper at home?
17. Do you borrow books from the public library?
18. Does anyone read at home?
19. What do they read?
20. Do you enjoy listening to your teacher read aloud?
21. Do your parents read to you?
22. Do they read to you in English or in another language?
23. Do you ever visit places and have things read to you, like religious stories?
24. Do you play games where you have to read, like Monopoly®?
25. What do you like to read—comic books, magazines, books?
26. Do you have a favorite book?
27. Do you have a favorite author?
28. Do you like long or short stories?
29. What kinds of stories bother you the most?
30. Could you tell me what it is like when you read at school?
31. What usually happens in your reading group?
32. Do you use the classroom library? The school library? When do you use them?
33. Do you like to read what your friends read?
34. Do you like to read aloud to other people?
35. Would you like to read to an older or younger reading buddy?
36. Do you discuss what you read with anyone?
37. Do you use a computer?
38. How much television do you watch each day?
39. What do you watch on television?
40. With whom do you watch television?
41. What do you like to do in your spare time?

42. Do you have any brothers or sisters?
43. Can they read?
44. Do they read?
45. If you had kids what would you read to them?
46. Who is the best reader that you know?
47. Who do you know that needs the most help reading?
48. How do your friends feel when you read aloud?
49. What kinds of words do you find difficult to read?
50. What do you do when you can't read a word?
51. What would you tell a friend to do if she or he couldn't read a word?
52. Do you look at the pictures in the books while you are reading?
53. What makes reading hard for you?
54. What would make it easier?
55. What can I do to make it easier for you to read?
56. What do you want to be when you grow up? What will you need to read to do that job?
57. Do you like to read some stories more than once?
58. What kind of a reading group are you in? Would you like to be in a different reading group?
59. Do you think textbooks are hard to read?
60. Do you borrow or trade books with your friends?
61. Do you have a book collection at home?
62. Do you print or cursive write?
63. What do you enjoy writing about?
64. Do you write letters to people?
65. Does anyone write to you?
66. Do you keep a journal?
67. How can your parents or teachers help you with your writing?
68. Do you play games on the computer?
69. Do you use a computer when you write?
70. Do you prefer to use a pen or a pencil?
71. What would you like to learn so that you can become a better writer?
72. What is something new you have learned to do in writing?
73. Do you ever write with someone else?
74. What is the best part of writing?
75. When you write, do you worry about making a spelling error?
76. What do you do when you're not sure how to write a word?
77. Do you ever use a dictionary?
78. What is your favorite toy?
79. Do you play sports?
80. Do you have heroes?

My Life as a Reader

Name:_____   Date:_____

1. How many books have you read in the past week/month? For each book, write the type (e.g., humor, history).

   _____

   _____

   _____

   _____

2. What interferes with your reading? How could you handle these problems?

   _____

   _____

3. Write the title of your favorite book, reasons why you liked it, and how you heard about it.

   _____

   _____

4. We've read many books aloud in class. What was your favorite read-aloud book? Why?

   _____

5. Write about three of the most important things you have learned through reading.

   _____

   _____

6. Describe the best conversation you ever had in a discussion group.

   _____

   _____

7. How much do you write about each book in your journal?

   _____

8. Think back to your favorite response about a book. Why was it your favorite response?

   _____

9. How would you describe yourself as a reader? As a writer?

   _____

   _____

10. List the goals for reading that you would like to meet by the end of the year.

   _____

   _____

11. How have you grown as a reader since the start of the year?

   _____

   _____

   _____

Benchmarks of Growth for the Emergent and Developing Reader

Name:_____   Date:_____

The reader:

1. Understands how books work.
   _____
   _____

2. Uses visual information to make and confirm predictions.
   _____
   _____

3. Checks that illustrations support print.
   _____
   _____

4. Uses details of illustrations to predict meaning.
   _____
   _____

5. Uses details of illustrations to predict some words.
   _____
   _____

6. Predicts logically upcoming events in the text.
   _____
   _____

7. Reads for meaning, moving easily through text.
   _____
   _____

8. Retells events in text.
   _____
   _____

9. Matches each spoken word to written word.
   _____
   _____

10. Can point to each word as it is spoken.
    _____
    _____

11. Uses known words to help solve new words.
    _____
    _____

12. Has a sight vocabulary of many words.

_____

_____

13. Pays attention to print.

_____

_____

14. Self-monitors by matching words and noting miscues.

_____

_____

15. Selects books at appropriate reading levels.

_____

_____

16. Enjoys and appreciates reading books.

_____

_____

Comments:

_____

_____

_____

_____

_____

_____

_____

_____

_____

_____

_____

_____

_____

_____

_____

Benchmarks of Growth for the Fluent and Independent Reader

Name:_____ Date:_____

The reader

1. Reads texts with increasingly difficult vocabulary, concepts, and structures.
   _____

2. Reads a range of genres, texts.
   _____

3. Interprets a text from a variety of perspectives.
   _____

4. Shows understanding of the characters in the text.
   _____

5. Reveals comprehension of a text through discussion.
   _____

6. Understands effects of stated and implied events in a text.
   _____

7. Appreciates the qualities of different writers — humour, sentiment, etc.
   _____

8. Can change genres easily (e.g., from fiction to memoir to historical).
   _____

9. Can read several pages of text at one sitting.
   _____

10. Maintains interest when reading a longer text.
    _____

11. Sustains interest in a text read over an extended period.
    _____

12. Returns easily to a text after other activities.
    _____

13. Reads critically and personally.
    _____

14. Reads fluently, particularly previously read texts.
    _____

15. Makes connections among texts.
    _____

16. Demonstrates an understanding of text through discussion and writing activities, and through art.
    _____

17. Summarizes or extends a text.

_____

18. Uses skills and strategies effectively while reading.

_____

19. Integrates information from all the cueing systems, while focusing on meaning.

_____

20. Determines meaning of increasingly difficult words without detracting from the flow of reading.

_____

21. Determines meaning of new words by analyzing them and then checking for meaning.

_____

22. Monitors meaning continuously while reading and self corrects.

_____

23. Rereads to check meaning.

_____

24. Uses text as reference for other curriculum areas.

_____

25. Finds information in texts, in both books and computers.

_____

26. Incorporates ideas from reading into writing.

_____

Comments:

_____
_____
_____
_____
_____
_____
_____
_____
_____
_____
_____

A Reading Profile

Name: _____   Date: _____

Does the young reader:

- experience and explore books that are well-written, at an appropriate level, and with significance to their lives and their literacy needs?

  _____

  _____

- know the purpose for reading each text?

  _____

  _____

- read texts with a variety of cultural connections?

  _____

  _____

- explore the ideas and features of a text before reading?

  _____

  _____

- recognize most words in the text quickly and automatically?

  _____

  _____

- uncover unfamiliar words in the text by making connections both to known words and patterns and to the context of the text?

  _____

  _____

- recognize the structure of the text as a way of making meaning?

  _____

  _____

- ask for support from peers, the teacher, or references when a complex problem arises?

  _____

  _____

- process new words by using them in other talking and writing situations?

  _____

  _____

- monitor their own comprehension and self-correct whenever possible?

  _____

  _____

- focus on meaning while they are reading?

  _____

  _____

- participate in a range of reading experiences — individually, in groups, and as a whole community?

  _____

  _____

- transfer what they are learning in reading to other curriculum areas?

  _____

  _____

- keep track of the books they have read and the activities they have completed?

  _____

  _____

- have access to books, both at school and at home?

  _____

  _____

- assess their growth as young readers, knowing the progress they have made, and the strategies that need to be strengthened?

  _____

  _____

Comments:

_____

_____

_____

_____

_____

_____

_____

_____

_____

_____

_____

_____

_____

_____

_____

_____

A Teacher's Checklist for Guided Reading

A. Time

1. Do I allow sufficient time for each group to read, reread and discuss a text together?

2. How much of the children's time is devoted to guided reading each day? Each week?

3. Have I built in enough time for observation and assessment of the children's progress?

4. Which aspect of the reading program receives most of my attention and time?

5. How much time, on average, do I spend with each group each day?

B. Texts

1. How many selections does each child read per week?

2. Do the texts reflect the children's interests and abilities?

3. Have I considered the effect of a text on the children's ideas and feelings?

4. Are texts organized adequately (e.g., grouped by level of difficulty)?

5. Do I have enough texts in my collection for the different abilities and interests of the children?

6. Have I been aware of the issues of equity and cultural representation in my text choices?

7. Does my text collection represent a range of genres?

8. Do the children participate in response and extension activities?

C. Groups

1. Are group sizes manageable?

   _____

2. Are groups reforming on a constant basis?

   _____

3. Am I spending significant time with each group during the week?

   _____

4. Are the children finding their group time useful and supportive?

   _____

5. Have I designed useful centres to encourage the children while I am conferring with a group or a child?

   _____

D. Instruction

1. Do I plan a prereading session to connect the children's experiences to the text and to introduce difficult concepts?

   _____

2. Do I give sufficient attention to the children who require conferences?

   _____

3. Are children acquiring and using strategies for making reading a successful experience?

   _____

4. Do children read the story silently? Do they read portions aloud?

   _____

5. Do they use the information from the illustrations to extend understanding?

   _____

6. Are children demonstrating competence in the use of strategies both while reading and after reading the text?

   _____

7. Do children monitor and correct errors while reading?

   _____

8. Do I assess the children with a running record when possible?

   _____

9. Do I adapt the guided reading program to fit the child's needs as a developing reader?

   _____

10. Do I focus on specific letter and word patterns using words from the text to promote growth in analyzing unfamiliar words?

    _____

11. Do the children retell the story after reading it?

12. Do I provide follow-up activities that ask the children to reflect upon the story to extend and support reading growth?

13. Do I give control of the reading to young readers?

14. Do I focus on new words in the text so that the children can acquire the necessary strategies for identifying them in future reading?

15. Do I listen to the children individually read aloud their texts and provide supportive comments to strengthen their rereadings?

16. Do I use pocket charts, word walls, and co-operative writing for instructional activities that support a young reader's reconstruction of the story?

17. Do I support positively the reading attempts of all children, confirming their predictions and assisting with their problem solving?

18. What types of errors does each child make? How is the child problem solving in attempting to self-correct?

E. **Assessing the Guided Reading Process**
  1. Did the children demonstrate an understanding of the text?

  2. Was the introductory activity useful in their attempts at meaning making?

  3. Did the child read aloud after reading silently, moving towards accuracy, phrasing, and fluency?

  4. How did each young reader use problem-solving strategies to understand text and cope with unfamiliar words?

  5. Was the text appropriate for the young readers?

Literature Circles

Name:_____ Date:_____

Group Behavior

The child

	Yes	No	Sometimes
• listens to others			
• doesn't interrupt others			
• values the contribution of other members			
• accepts another's opinion			
• helps to extend the discussion			
• enjoys working as part of a group			
• shares opinions willingly			

Reading

The child

	Yes	No	Sometimes
• reads required materials			
• uses strategies to tackle new words and concepts			
• uses illustration as an aid to comprehension			
• understands sections of the text that are challenging			
• draws conclusions based on what she or he has read			
• relates the text to others she or he has read			

Writing

The child

	Yes	No	Sometimes
• uses his or her journal to record reflections, questions, puzzles			
• makes predictions			
• identifies topics to be pursued in discussion groups			
• summarizes material read accurately			
• relates text to previous knowledge and experience			
• extends knowledge from the text			

Speaking

The child

	Yes	No	Sometimes
• supports opinion with material from text			
• recognizes the validity of others' statements			
• participates voluntarily in the discussion			

Other Comments:

_____

_____

_____

Self-Assessment: Literature Circles

Name:_____   Date:_____

	Yes	No	Sometimes
1. I was prepared for today's reading.			
2. I listened to my group members.			
3. I made contributions to the group's discussion.			
4. I asked questions about the book.			
5. I shared my opinion about the book.			
6. I changed my opinion about the book based on the discussion.			
7. I helped the group solve problems.			
8. I was able to retell parts of the story.			
9. I commented on the author's style and use of language.			
10. I referred to the book to support my point of view.			
11. I related the book to my own experiences.			
12. I developed a better understanding of the book because the literature circle.			
13. I recorded some special words and phrases to remember and use.			
14. I enjoy working in literature circles.			
15. I learn about myself by participating in a literature circle.			

My strengths in literature circles include:

_____

_____

_____

Areas I still need to work on include:

_____

_____

_____

My most valuable contribution to the group today was:

_____

_____

_____

Group Assessment of Literature Circles

Our discussion of this book was _____

because we _____

My participation was _____

because I _____

Our discussions helped me understand this book in these ways:

a) _____

_____

b) _____

_____

c) _____

_____

d) _____

_____

These topics were still not clear to me after we finished our discussions:

a) _____

_____

b) _____

_____

c) _____

_____

d) _____

_____

This discussion would have been more helpful if we

_____

_____

_____

On a scale of 1 (low) to 5 (high) I would rate this literature circle as (circle one);

1   2   3   4   5

My Reading Log

Name: _____

Title of Book	Date Finished	Comments
1.		
2.		
3.		
4.		
5.		
6.		
7.		
8.		
9.		
10.		
11.		
12.		
13.		
14.		
15.		
16.		
17.		
18.		
19.		
20.		
21.		
22.		
23.		
24.		
25.		
26.		
27.		
28.		
29.		
30.		
31.		
32.		
33.		
34.		
35.		
36.		
37.		
38.		
39.		
40.		

A Plot Organizer

Name: _____   Story Outline For: _____

Author: _____   Publisher: _____   Date: _____

Setting/Main Characters

Story Theme

The Problem

Story Sequence

1.

2.

3.

Factors Affecting Comprehension

The Child

- an interest in and appreciation of the text
- connections the child makes to the text from both life and literacy experiences
- familiarity with the ideas that will be represented in the text
- awareness of the characteristics of the genre (e.g., report, novel, poem)
- feelings of success and competence as a reader
- an understanding of the goal for reading a particular text selection
- responsability for choosing the text to be read
- opportunities for responding to the text through discussion, writing, etc.
- the attributes, opinions and behaviors of peers during reading activities
- the conditions surrounding the event: a private reading experience, a collaborative experience, a public shared experience, a performance, or a test
- the time limits for accomplishing the reading

The Teacher

- pretext support for setting the stage for reading
- careful selection of the material for interest and ability
- giving a sense of ownership of the reading experience to the child
- building motivating process for engaging the reader in the activity
- designing an organization that supports intensive and extensive reading
- regular monitoring of young readers in order to help them
- offering prompts as strategies used to support the young reader while reading the text
- supporting independent reading (e.g., a tape of the book)
- developing the teacher's relationship with the young reader (e.g., tester, mentor, fascilitator)
- creating follow-up activities that promote reflections , rereading, or revisiting of the text

The Text

- qualities of the language of the text that encourage a particular reader
- genre of the text (e.g., narrative, lists) that was selected
- the complexity of ideas presented in the text for the particular reader
- the demand on the reader's background experience
- the inference load on the reader
- the level of the vocabulary (e.g., unfamiliar words, context)
- the illustrations that support the experience of the text
- the skill of the writer in involving the reader and in presenting ideas in meaningful and well crafted text

Evaluating Your Reading Program

A. Connecting Reading and Learning
- Are the children excited about the reading program in your class?
- Do all the children feel successful in their reading progress?
- Do the children draw on personal experiences to help them understand a text?
- Do the children see one another as readers?
- Do they value their reading and writing activities as useful and significant in their learning?
- Do the children recommend books to their peers?
- Do the children have opportunities to reflect upon their reading experiences?
- Do the children have ample opportunity to respond to what they have read? To share their responses?
- Do the children value others' experiences as a means of understanding their own reading of a text?
- Do the children treat one another with respect during book discussions?
- Do both you and the children offer positive and helpful feedback?
- Are you a good model for your students?
- Do you value reading in your life?
- Do you make time to read in your life?
- Do you as a teacher talk about your personal reading?
- Do you read professional books and articles, and share them with colleagues?
- Do you provide effective demonstrations, responding to the needs of the students?
- How do you feel about the conferences you organize, the whole-class shared experiences, and your literacy groups?
- Do you know each child's reading history?
- Do you respect all the young readers in your class?
- How does your literacy program affect curriculum learning in other areas?
- Do you encourage children to take ownership of their reading?
- Do the children take responsibility for the activities they choose to complete?
- Have you shared your expectations for each child with each child?
- How do you assist those readers in difficulty?
- Have you shared with the children how they will be assessed?
- Are the children participating in self-assessment about their reading growth?
- Do your assessment and evaluation practices reflect your instructional practices?
- What changes will you make in your literacy program next year?
- Do you communicate effectively with parents and the school community about your program?
- What benchmarks for reading does your school have in place?

B. Teacher Reading Aloud
- How often do you read to the whole class? To a group?
- How are the books for reading aloud selected?
- Do you read parts of books aloud, as well as other items (e.g., samples from your journal, letters)?
- Do guests read aloud to the class? Are tapes used?
- How do you arrange the room for reading aloud?
- Do you allow questions and comments by the children during the reading?
- Does the class participate in activities after listening to the reading aloud?
- Do you present book talks about new books that will be in the classroom and in the school library?
- Do children read orally to the class after rehearsing? How do you establish a safe context?
- Do children volunteer to present book talks to the class?
- Do you later record observations regarding children's participation and behavior during your reading aloud times?

C. Shared Reading
- What materials are available for shared reading?
- Do children compose/read transcribed or dictated stories/information?
- Do you incorporate big book formats for shared reading?
- Do you prepare charts and overhead transparencies?
- What techniques do you employ during shared reading to demonstrate effective reading strategies?
- Do the children retell the source after the shared reading?
- In what response activities do the children participate?
- Do you use cloze or masking activities to promote prediction and word choice?
- How do you focus on word knowledge and sentence structure during shared reading occasions?
- Are small versions of the large text available after the shared reading for children to read independently?
- Do children model patterns in their writing on their shared reading experiences?
- Do you demonstrate reading strategies with/for the class during the shared reading time?
- Is there an abundance of familiar children's literature used in the shared reading, much of it containing rhythmic or predictable language?
- Are children invited to participate in the shared reading as members of the classroom community?
- Do you revisit selections again throughout the year, adding to the reading repertoire of the children?

D. Independent Reading by Children
- Is there a wide selection of books for children?
- Do the books in the class represent a range of roles for both genders?
- Do the books represent a range of cultures, both by author and within the content?
- How are the books organized for selection for independent reading?
- How do you assist children in selecting books?
- What is your role during independent reading time?
- Do the children draw from their reading for other learning activities?
- Do children take books home for reading to parents?
- Do you prepare a book talk about new and different books each week?
- Is the library involved in your independent reading program?
- How do the children keep track of what has been read?
- Do the children engage in response and extension activities?
- Do you have the children identify the purpose for their reading?
- Do you find opportunities for interviewing children or for assisting children in difficulty?
- Do you use reading journals or dialogue journals with the children?

E. Group Reading
- Does each child in the group read the same book?
- How are materials selected?
- Do children read the text silently?
- What oral reading do they engage in after reading?
- Do other children call out words or wait for the reader to attempt them?
- What is your role during the group reading?
- Is a taped version of the selection used for some children?
- Do you cut apart words or sentences or paragraphs for children to sequence after the reading?
- Do you find opportunities for extending phonic strategies?
- Do the children examine syntactic structures?
- Do the children engage in co-operative meaning-making discussions?

- Are extension activities carried out by the children — book talks, retelling, drama, writing, research, games, singing?
- Are follow-up activities leading to further enjoyment and engagement with the text?
- How often do you work with each group during the week?
- Do you vary your instruction, from demonstrations to mini-lessons for selected children?
- How are the children grouped? In a variety of ways?
- Do children read aloud their writing that was generated by the text?
- Do you participate in group conferences?
- Do children interact with their peers? Work with a partner?
- Do children work with a buddy from another grade?
- Do you tape or transcribe the children's discussions for later analysis?
- Do you create opportunities for interest-based, multiability reading groups?
- Do you create opportunities for needs-based groups?
- Do you promote opportunities for noncompetitive shared learning activities and games?

F. Assisting a Young Reader
- Do you use engaging books with a predictable text that will support the reader?
- Are there prereading activities before the child interacts with the book?
- Is vocabulary taught in context during and after reading, or in isolation before reading?
- Do you read to or with the child?
- Does the child read the book silently?
- Does the child read aloud to you?
- What strategies do you use to assist the child while reading?
- How do you help the child with words that are unknown or difficult to read?
- Do you give each child sufficient wait time and encouragement to figure out words and meanings independently?
- Are you guiding children to apply the strategies that effective readers use?
- Are you helping foster independence?
- How do you draw a child's attention to phonic patterns? Are there extension activities that focus on these patterns?
- What syntactic structures do you draw attention to?
- Does the child retell the story?
- Does the child reconstruct the story using word/sentence cards?
- What story ideas does the child discuss?
- Are you asking important questions that follow naturally from the text?
- What writing grows from the story?
- Does the child have opportunities to reread the text, building fluency?

G. Connecting Writing and Reading
- Does the child write for a variety of purposes?
- Do you confer with the child about ideas, structure, and transcription skills?
- Does the child keep a journal, notebook, or log?
- Do you respond in writing to the child's responses?
- Does the child use his or her written work for other activities?
- Do you present a variety of ideas for publishing books?
- Do you utilize volunteers to help the child revise, edit, and publish personal books?
- Do you demonstrate or teach mini-lessons drawn from the children's written work?
- How do you allow inventive spelling and still promote standard English spelling?
- Do you assess the child's developmental stage of spelling?
- Do you provide a print-rich environment with resources for promoting spelling growth?
- Do you draw words from the stories to explore in various ways — the delights of language, the patterns, the irregularities?

A Suggested Guide for Young Readers

1. Selecting your reading materials

Successful readers read lots of books! Sometimes you need a novel that is easy and fun to read; sometimes you need an information book that is at your level; sometimes you need a computer article that is challenging to read. You can build book lists for the year by talking to other children, discussing your situation with the teacher, visiting the library, checking reviews in magazines and newspapers, and using the computer network on screen.

2. Reading what your friends read

When you are reading the same novel as a group of classmates, you can talk about the story, listen to what others are thinking, predict what you think may happen next, and be surprised about, and interested in, the interpretations that your group members share.

3. Abandoning a book you have selected

Sometimes your choice of book is not suitable, and you have to decide if you should choose another one, or get some help in understanding the one you are having difficulty with. Think about these questions:
- Do you need more background information about the book to help you?
- Are there too many difficult words that interfere with the meaning making?
- Have you given the book a fair trial?

4. Understanding the kind of text you are reading

Each kind of print requires that you read in a particular way. A reference book, such as an encyclopedia or a computer article, may require you to skim the text until you find the information you need. You may need to read a poem several times (perhaps aloud) until you can find the clues the poet gives about how the words should be read. A long novel may mean that you need to pause after a few chapters and discuss the events with a classmate or the teacher. You can begin to discover the patterns an author uses in writing different types of books.

5. Using the parts of a book

Often the table of contents, the author's notes, information about the author on the back cover, the chapter titles, the end summary, or the index at the end of the book can assist you in seeing how the book works, so that you can get the most from reading it.

6. After you have read a book

Thinking about a book you have read can help you to better understand the goal of the author, as well as how you really feel about the book. Sometimes you will want to record your thoughts and feelings as you are reading in your journal. Later, you can select a portion to reuse in other ways – as the source of a poem, as a painting, or as a retelling of the story from a personal viewpoint. It may happen that revisiting the story may change your original opinion of it.

7. Recommending books

You may want to share your responses to a book or an article with a friend. Perhaps you can add to the discussion of the theme, or your poem written about one of the characters can help other readers to better understand the story. One of the best ways to find a good book to read is to listen to book talks by your friends.

8. Reading unfamiliar words

You need to develop strategies for figuring out a word in the book that you don't know. Sometimes you can find out a word from the meaning within the story; other times you may have to look at the word carefully to see if you can understand parts of the word, or recognize a group of letters such as a prefix. While reading, a name can be referred to as Mr. Z_____ until you find out in the discussion how to pronounce it. You can omit other words if they are not necessary for the meaning at the moment, or you can look up a significant word in a reference book.

9. Connecting your reading and your writing

What you have read can be a source for what you may want to write. Good writers read all the time – looking for ideas, patterns, words, phrases, special ways of trying to put thought down on paper. Borrow from other authors and hitchhike on different print ideas.

10. Connecting your reading to other subjects

Read the materials in your other subjects as you do in reading class, as ideas written by authors who have something important to say. You could find an article "on line" that discusses what your textbook is talking about to help you hear "the story" of the topic you are exploring. For example, if you are studying a particular country, you could read a novel set there, read letters on the web from those who live there, or read a book of poems from a writer who knows the people and the place. Reading is an act of understanding, of making meaning, no matter the subject, the timetable, or the topic.

11. Keeping a reading log

You need to keep a record of what you have read throughout the year to demonstrate to your classmates, your teacher, and your parents your literacy development, as well as reminding yourself of your achievements. It may be useful as well to record the types of response activities you have completed with each book. Some children collect these reading logs for the whole of their school years and use them in their portfolios for entrance to high school.

12. Reading at home

Continue to read outside school. Make time to build print power on the school bus, before bed, Sunday after dinner when you may want a quiet time, when you feel tired or lonely (or even lazy), when it is raining (or snowing), when you are in trouble, or when you are waiting at the dentist. People who come to enjoy reading do so because they make reading a priority in their lives.

13. Reading anything and everything

Read anything and everything – your private time is your own (TV Guide, comics, novels, magazines, newspapers - don't forget to count computer print).

14. Skimming and Scanning

Try to time yourself: how long does it take you to read a page of an information book? Could you skim more than you do? Could you scan to find the information you need? Do you skip parts that aren't necessary to your making sense of what you are reading? (Good readers know all of these tricks.)

15. Connecting your life to your reading

Each book you read should connect to others you have read, to a film you saw, or perhaps to an experience in your life. You build life connections, even to a story that is completely unlike anything you have known. Somehow, you are inside the book looking out, and you are changed forever.

16. Seeing yourself as a reader

Learn to know yourself as a reader, your style of reading, how you interact with certain authors, how you can understand why you respond in a certain way, how a particular book fits in with your growing picture of yourself.

Parents of Primary/Junior Students

Name:_____ Child's Name:_____ Date:_____

Does your child:
- enjoy stories read aloud by family members?
- enjoy reading aloud to you?
- enjoy reading independently?
- read signs for streets, store names, restaurant chains, advertisements?
- read for a longer period of time than she or he did several months ago?
- choose books that she or he can read independently?
- choose a variety of books to read (e.g. humor, mystery)?
- make predictions about the text?
- talk about a book in relation to another (e.g. This book is like _____ because _____)?
- talk about a book in relation to himself or herself?
- relate to characters in a book?
- enjoy talking about a text during and after reading it?
- use pictures as clues to the story's plot?
- try to figure out new words independently?
- skip a word, then come back to it later?
- analyze the word by saying aloud the letter sounds?
- make logical guesses for words she or he doesn't know?
- ask for help after she or he has tried to solve it independently?

Other Comments:

_____

_____

_____

Changes You Have Noticed in Your Child's Reading Behavior:

_____

_____

_____

Areas of Concern:

_____

_____

_____

Parents of Intermediate Students

Name:_____ Child's name:_____ Date:_____

Does your child:

	Yes	No	Sometimes
read on different occasions?			
read a variety of different types of books (e.g., time travel stories, mysteries, war stories)?			
have a favorite type of story?			
read newspapers and magazines?			
share his or her opinion of material read?			
write about what she or he has read?			
find information independently by using the Internet, the local library?			
persist in reading when the text is challenging?			
take risks in learning (e.g., reading about a new topic, selecting a difficult book)?			
learn from past mistakes in reading and writing?			
see himself/herself as a successful reader?			

Other Comments:

_____

_____

_____

_____

Changes You Have Noticed in Your Child's Reading Behavior:

_____

_____

_____

Areas of Concern:

_____

_____

_____

Index